Small Business Computers for First-Time Users

I R Beaman

PUBLISHED BY NCC PUBLICATIONS

British Library Cataloguing in Publication Data

Beaman, I. R.
   Small business computers for first-time users.
   1. Business – Data processing
   2. Electronic digital computers
   I. Title
   001.64   HF5548.2

ISBN 0-85012-374-7

© THE NATIONAL COMPUTING CENTRE LIMITED, 1983

All rights reserved. No part of this publication may be reproduced, stored in a retrieval system, or transmitted, in any form or by an means, without the prior permission of The National Computing Centre.

First published in 1983 by:

NCC Publications, The National Computing Centre Limited, Oxford Road, Manchester M1 7ED, England.

Typeset in 10pt Times Roman and printed by UPS Blackburn Limited, 76-80 Northgate, Blackburn, Lancashire.

ISBN 0-85012-374-7

Contents

	Page
Preface	

PART 1 GUIDELINES

1	**Introduction**	13
	The First-Time User's Dilemma	13
	The Approach Adopted	13
2	**Computer Appreciation**	17
	Introduction	17
	Hardware	17
	Software	23
	A Typical Installation	27
	Summary	37
3	**The Feasibility Study**	39
	Introduction	39
	The Aim of the Study	41
	Retaining a Consultant?	44
	The Detailed Study	49
	Analysing the Results	58
	The Study Report	59
4	**Going Out To Tender**	61
	Introduction	61
	The Tender Document	61
	Selecting a List of Suppliers	64

5 Evaluating the Proposals — 69

Introduction — 69
Evaluation of Costs — 70
Analysis of System Features — 70
Allocation of Weights — 72
Extraction of System Features from the Proposals — 75
Scoring of System Features — 82
Selection of the Best Solution — 83
The Evaluation Report — 83

6 Implementation — 87

Introduction — 87
Contract Options — 88
Software Package Contracts — 88
Systems Development Contracts — 89
Hardware Contracts — 90
Typical Contract Contents — 90
Stages of the Implementation Plan — 92

PART 2 COMMON TYPES OF COMPUTER APPLICATIONS

7 Payroll — 103

Introduction — 103
The Payroll Files — 105
Input to the Payroll System — 107
Reports from the Payroll System — 110

8 Sales Ledger — 115

Introduction — 115
Types of Accounts — 116
Computerising the Sales Ledger — 118

9 Purchase Ledger — 127

Introduction — 127
Input to the System — 128
The Purchase Ledger System — 130
Manual Procedures in Cheque Processing — 138

10 Sales Order Processing   139

   Introduction   139
   Input to the System   140
   The System Files   141
   The Order Processing System   145
   Possible Extensions   147

11 Nominal Ledger   153

   Introduction   153
   Input to the System   155
   The Nominal Ledger System   156
   The Company Chart of Accounts   163

Appendices

   1 Sample Study Questionnaires   169
   2 Cost Elements of Computer Systems   179
   3 Sample Study Report   183
   4 Specimen Tender Document   199
   5 Suggested Letter to Suppliers   211
   6 Glossary of Terms   241

Preface

This book is designed to help the small business through the various stages involved in computerisation. It is also designed to remove much of the mystique associated with anything related to computers. It is intended as a tool to help people to help themselves. This does not mean that there are not stages in the computerisation process where the professional experience and knowledge of a consultant may be required. What it does mean is that with the help of this book, you, the first-time user, can successfully undertake the daunting task of deciding which computer to install and ensure that the implementation runs smoothly.

It is meant as a supplement, rather than an alternative, to asking sales representatives from various computing suppliers to come in and explain their particular system. What the first-time user really wants is unbiased information in a format that will assist the evaluation of computing needs, and of the ability of each supplier to satisfy them.

Alternatively you could hire a consultant, but how would you go about selecting him? You still do not have enough knowledge of computing to evaluate the consultant's integrity and ability. What is more, consultants can be rather expensive.

If at this point you admit that you really do not know enough about computers, either to make a valid analysis of what a computer can do for you, or to choose the best computer system for your needs, then you have taken a first solid step forward. You have also avoided the trap that so many first-time users fall into, which is to take the 'easy' way out, suggesting to themselves that anything having to do with a computer is highly technical and therefore something that they should not be concerned with.

At any rate, with the realisation of what you don't know and what you need to know, you are now ready to take your second positive step forward.

PART 1

Guidelines

1 Introduction

THE FIRST-TIME USER'S DILEMMA

So you are thinking of installing a computer system! Since the computer is surrounded with an aura of mystique, the first-time user is both intrigued and baffled at the prospect of deciding whether or not to recommend a computer. All of this is compounded by the fact that he has often been misled into believing that the computer is far too technical to understand, and as a consequence leaves the decision in the hands of small external accountants or other so-called 'experts'.

Nothing could be more hazardous. First of all, the first-time user must understand that a computer, in essence, is no more complicated than any other system. The computer is one of the greatest tools developed by man. It can be, in a sense, compared to a motor car, also a powerful tool. It is true that keeping a car in repair often requires a highly skilled mechanic. Operating it, however, can be mastered by everyone. Operating a computer system is more complicated than operating a car, but not nearly as complicated as many first-time users have been led to believe.

THE APPROACH ADOPTED

Each of the following steps to effective computer implementation is discussed in a separate chapter:

    The Feasibility Study

    Going out to Tender

    Evaluating the Proposals

    Implementation

The first decision that you are faced with is whether to investigate the *feasibility* of the project – Can your objectives be achieved? With what type of system? Will it be economically viable? Some assume that considering a computer is sufficient justification for acquiring one. This is rarely the case. This does not mean that the decision to go ahead and investigate feasibility should be taken lightly. You are probably committing a senior person in your company to a very detailed investigation which will take up a lot of time and require a level of understanding of systems investigation and design.

At this stage you should weigh these factors against the direct costs of retaining a consultant to assist you in this exercise. The 'free' alternative is to invite one or two suppliers to do the survey for you. You may think you know what you want to achieve; the supplier knows only what he can supply, but you do not yet know how to achieve your objectives or whether any computer-based solution will be viable, let alone whether this particular supplier's system is suitable.

If the feasibility study produces a positive recommendation to proceed with the installation of a computer system, then this is tantamount to asking you to make a decision in principle that the type of solution recommended is right for your company and that now is the time to act. The question then becomes 'Which computer?'. Again the services of a suitable consultant can save much wasted time at this stage. Even if you decide to undertake the evaluation of supplier's proposals yourself, you should use the professional consultant's selection process – provide potential suppliers with a written *invitation to tender* and evaluate their proposals on a checklist basis.

Even if a consultant has been retained to undertake the *evaluation of the proposals,* you cannot expect him to make the actual selection decision for you. The important step is ensuring that the right suppliers get on to your shortlist and that *you* make the actual selection decision, based on a Balance Sheet of pros and cons for each shortlisted proposal. Supplier selection must be based on the objective evaluation already carried out, but will often hinge on how you choose to weight the importance of the less tangible and more subjective factors – Who really understands our situation? Which supplier makes me confident of his ability to make his proposals work? This is obviously a decision that cannot be rushed; you can afford to resist the pressures from inside the company and from the suppliers – you have taken steps to ensure that it is indeed *your* decision.

Eventually, having signed contracts, you may heave a sigh of relief. Yet this is a dangerous time – there is a strong temptation now to turn the problems of making your chosen system work over to somebody else 'with more time', or even worse, leave the whole *implementation* of the computer system up to the supplier. Nothing could be worse. Unless you are actively involved in monitoring progress on the achievement of your systems objectives and on the supplier's performance, it is unlikely that the project will be successful. The successful implementation of the required systems within budget and on time requires the user and the supplier to work closely together.

There will come a time, or more likely a number of occasions, when your satisfaction has to be explicit – Are we satisfied that this particular system meets our specified requirements? Can we now accept it under the terms of the contract? The same rigorous procedure must apply as in all the earlier stages, especially in accepting changes and making any payment to the supplier. Once you are satisfied that everything that was contracted for has been supplied and that the systems are fully operational then congratulations are certainly in order. Unfortunately it is rarely as easy to be entirely confident that what you have got is indeed working satisfactorily, and really only time will tell. If everything does go smoothly, it is still good practice to review the performance of the systems periodically and appraise any proposed new work for the computer on the same detailed basis.

2 Computer Appreciation

INTRODUCTION

Electronic computers have been in existence in some form or other since the mid-1940s; and for most people they used to be regarded as large, expensive machines ideal for doing very complex calculations quickly or for carrying out repetitive, routine tasks on a massive scale, but suitable only for the very largest organisations.

But over the last decade the technology has dramatically changed; and with it the computer. Many computers today can be sited on a desk or in the corner of an office, with their cost very much less than that of an executive motor car.

This breakthrough in scale and cost means that for the first time many small organisations are able to justify computers for their routine tasks: order processing; production scheduling; sales and purchase ledgers; payroll and the like. However, many small organisations have been deterred by the baffling range of available computer systems; and by the jargon of the computer people with their hardware, software, bits and bytes. These circumstances have made what is basically a relatively straightforward topic seem much more complicated than it really is.

Here, we hope to dispel some of that mystique, first of all by explaining the basic elements of the equipment itself; and then by describing some of the applications for which it can be used.

HARDWARE

First of all let us explain the terms 'hardware' and 'software'. All the mechanical and electronic equipment which goes to make up a computer is referred to as the hardware; the programs of instructions, some of which may be supplied with the hardware, or those which the user writes himself, are the software. The computer, like any other mechanical device, is unable to function unless someone starts operating it. In the case of the computer, one of the first actions of the operator is to load a program which contains the instructions for its next job; this could be to make it start printing invoices, for example. Of course, someone will have spent many weeks or months writing this program before it is loaded onto the computer.

Input

The programs and all the transactions and records upon which the computer has to perform its calculations have to be presented to the computer by someone operating an input device. Very often it is something which looks just like a typewriter keyboard attached to the computer.

The most common form of input device on small computers is the visual display unit (VDU). This has a typewriter keyboard with a small televi-

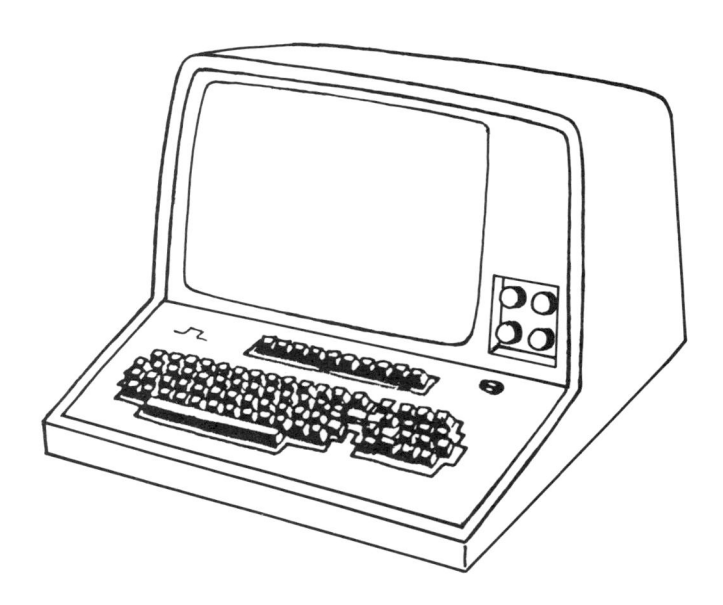

Figure 2.1 Visual Display Unit (VDU)

sion screen above it (Figure 2.1). The operator keys in the appropriate information (data) and an image of what is typed appears on the screen. In many instances the computer is programmed to check what is input so that it can 'prompt' the operator if a mistake seems to have been made. For example, if the operator keys in a part number which does not appear in the computer's pre-stored catalogue of parts the computer can display "PART NO. INVALID" on the screen. The operator can then make a correction.

The VDUs and other types of terminal are connected to the computer by cable or by normal BT telephone lines. When a key is pressed, the signal is converted to a form suitable for relaying down the telephone line (rather like the Morse code) and then converted into a form suitable for holding in the central computer when the message is received. VDUs can be adjacent to or sited many miles away from the central computer (but of course distance can add to the cost). More than one VDU can be linked to a single computer, but there may be limitations on certain machines which you would be wise to find out before planning your system.

There are other methods of preparing data for input, eg punched card, key-to-disk and paper tape. These methods tend to be associated with fairly big computer installations where there is a need to prepare large amounts of data prior to batch processing. Sometimes input is from documents which have another use, like bank cheques, whose magnetic ink figures are capable of being read directly into the computer once the document has served its normal purpose.

Central Processing Unit (CPU)

Once data has been accepted by the computer it is transferred into the CPU or memory. Originally composed of thermionic valves, then transistors, now the CPU is likely to consist of a tiny silicon chip no bigger than a fingernail on which are inscribed thousands of individual circuits. Each circuit can be switched to one of two states, representing 1 or 0 and usually referred to as 'BITS' (short for binary digit). With eight of these bits strung together, any number or letter of the alphabet and numerous other symbols can be represented in binary form. A configuration of eight bits is usually referred to as a 'BYTE' especially in IBM equipment. Other manufacturers talk about 'characters' of memory, which generally correspond to the IBM byte. A small business computer will have between 32,000 (32K) and 256,000 (256K) bytes or characters of memory.

Also contained in the central processor is the control unit where program instructions are executed and the arithmetic unit where calculations are performed.

The basic speed of each hardware operation is known as the 'cycle time'. Cycle times for most modern machines are usually quoted in nanoseconds (thousand millionths of a second). It follows, therefore, that the computer can perform millions of calculations in the time it takes the human operator to press one key on the keyboard of the VDU.

File Storage

Because the CPU is limited in size, the computer usually requires some further storage capability to record all the information and programs needed to complete a typical commercial system. For instance, if the computer was carrying out the job of printing out name and address labels for a thousand customers, it would probably only be able to hold one or two names and addresses in its memory at any one time. The program would have to 'read' these names and addresses in the CPU one or two at a time from a file storage facility and print them out until the CPU was free to accept one or two more, and so on. The most common form of file storage facility on the small computer is the disk. These disks are similar in concept to those bought in the music shop, the data on them being inscribed in 'bit' patterns in circular tracks about the surface. They usually come in 'disk packs' containing several disks, with each disk pack holding anything from 5 million up to several hundred million bytes of information. (A million bytes is called a megabyte.) These disks are usually exchangeable, so that further information can be held on reserve disks, and only fixed to the computer when actually required. Once fixed, information can be 'read' or transferred from the disk to the CPU in milliseconds (ie thousands of characters per second).

Other forms of backing store found on minicomputers are diskettes (sometimes called 'floppy' disks). These are smaller units of storage consisting of a single flexible disk in an envelope (about the size of a '45' record) which can be inserted into a special device attached to the computer. The tape cassette (exactly like a music cassette) is also used.

Like their musical counterparts, when we 'read' or play disks, tapes, etc, the information which is contained on them remains undisturbed, and they can be used thousands of times before wearing out. If we want to overwrite any part of their contents we can do so by assembling the new

COMPUTER APPRECIATION 21

information in the CPU and 'writing' it to the disk or tape, just as you would record over something on your domestic tape recorder.

The size of file storage required by the user obviously depends on the number of files that he wishes to retain. This varies from application to application, but essentially the same files are maintained in a computer system as in the manual system. For example, in a payroll system a record needs to be kept of each employee including such things as employee number, name, pay rate, etc. This information is collected together in the form of a payroll record, and these records together form the payroll 'master' file.

Thus computer files are made up of records, and records consist of associated items of information about the same entity (sometimes called 'fields'). Master files are those containing records with permanent or semi-permanent information such as the payroll file above. Timesheet data on the other hand, showing employee number and hours worked during a particular pay period would, by its very nature, be short-lived, and would therefore be stored on a 'transaction' file. This file would most probably be cleared at the end of the pay period after the period totals had been added to the master file.

A first approximation therefore in determining the amount of file storage required would be the volume of information recorded on master and transaction files in the manual applications. Further details on this topic can be found in Chapter 3 under 'The Study Report'.

Output

The computer requires some form of output to present its results to the user. If a simple enquiry is all that is needed, then this can usually be displayed on a VDU. For example, if a customer wants to know if a certain stock item is available, the VDU operator can key in the Part number of the item and the answer will come back on the screen.

If 'hard copy' is required, then a character printer or line printer is needed. Character printers print character-by-character rather like typewriters, attaining speeds of up to 200 characters per second (cps).

The line printer waits till a whole line of print is assembled in the CPU and then prints it all out in one burst, a line at a time. Speeds of 300 lines per minute (1pm) are common on small computers, although much higher speeds can be attained on large computers.

Some VDUs have hard-copy attachments which enable the user to take a copy of the VDU display, when required.

Other specialised forms of output which can be obtained include the graphics terminal and digital plotter. The graphics terminal displays information on a screen in graphical form and the digital plotter performs the same function but provides hard copy of the chart, drawing or blueprint for the user.

The tapes, disks, cassettes, etc, described under 'file storage' can also be considered as output; and could be a useful way of transferring data from one computer system to another.

Summary

Every computer may be regarded as including the following components (Figure 2.2):

INPUT DEVICE:	Some means of feeding information into the system.
CENTRAL PROCESSOR:	The area that information is transferred to for programs to be performed and for calculations to be carried out.
FILE STORAGE:	Tapes, disks, etc, which provide bulk storage areas for the user's records.
OUTPUT DEVICE:	Some means of displaying or printing out results.

A pocket calculator, in contrast to a computer, has no backing store. Usually its central processor is limited, so that the user has to key in the program step-by-step. However, there is an input device (the keyboard); a processor; and an output device (the display). So if you had a very powerful pocket calculator in which you could store long programs of instructions instead of keying them in step-by-step, and you were able to attach to it a cassette recorder on which you could hold all the data that you wanted to process, instead of keying that in laboriously by hand, then you would have a very small and simple computer.

COMPUTER APPRECIATION

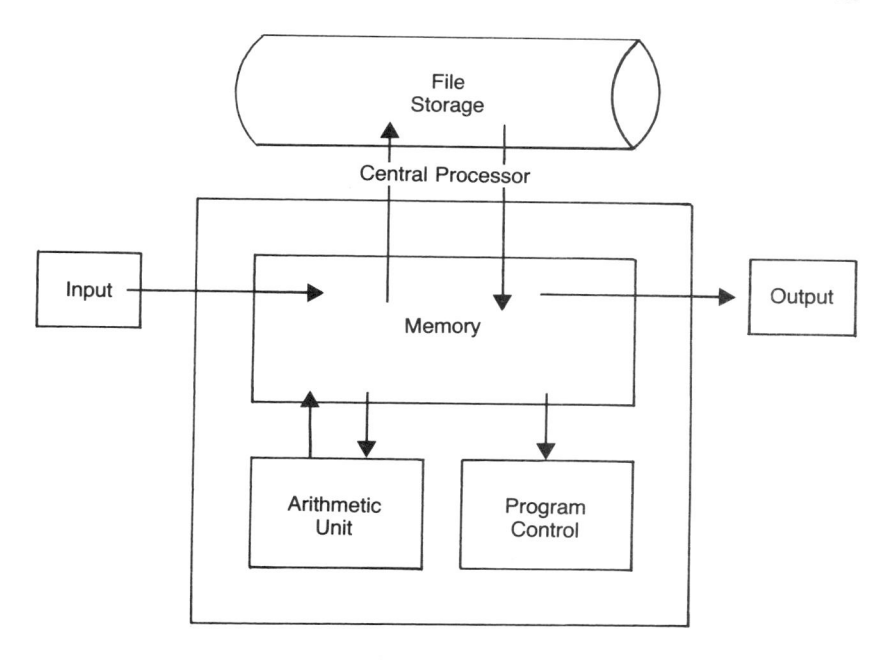

Figure 2.2 Basic Elements of a Computer

SOFTWARE

This refers to all the programs of instructions which make the computer operable. There are various software classifications:

Operating Systems

The computer supplier will normally provide programs which control input, output and the running of the applications programs. On some small computers the operating system is only capable of running one application at a time (single-user operating system). On larger computers the operating system is more sophisticated and enables several users to access the machine at the same time. In this case the operating system will share the processor time and computer resources between the various users and the applications which they are using. For instance, if USER A is making a stock enquiry and USER B wants to update stock, the operating system ensures that each user is allocated a portion of time, and each appropriate program is brought into the CPU so that the desired task can be carried out. This is usually so organised that each user thinks he has the sole use of the computer; for as the switches between programs and between users take microseconds, there is no apparent delay.

Programming Languages

The user can write his own programs in one of a number of different programming languages. Some of the popular ones provided on small computers are: COBOL, RPG, BASIC, ALGOL, CORAL and FORTRAN. Many of these can be used on more than one different type of computer, and so a 'compiler' or 'assembler' is provided to translate these languages ('user code') into the language of the computer ('machine code'). The choice of language is governed firstly by what compilers are available for your chosen computer; by the nature of the language (some are like plain English, some like mathematical formulae, and therefore will be chosen according to the nature of the problem); and finally by personal preference (if you find BASIC is easy to use, then that is likely to be your chosen language).

Applications Packages

Instead of writing your own programs from scratch, packages (ie standard pre-written programs) for most of the standard commercial applications, such as Payroll, Sales Ledger, and the like, can be obtained from many suppliers. It may be that these packages produce an end-product which is not entirely in line with your present mode of working. For example, the sales ledger package may produce a different layout of statement from that to which you are normally accustomed. You must weigh up the disadvantages inherent in the package with the cost of writing your own system from scratch. If the package costs say, £5,000, this is probably equivalent to six man-months' program writing and testing time; which is likely to be the minimum time taken to write any major computer application.

As a rule of thumb, therefore, the small computer user would expect to buy most of his major computer applications from the supplier; and only if his application were unique or if he wished to carry out a number of short 'one-off' operations would he attempt to write his own programs.

COMPUTER APPRECIATION

Tailor-Made Packages

There is another alternative. If there are no packages immediately available, and the user feels unsure of writing his own, he could contract out to the supplier, or to an independent software house, who would undertake to write the necessary programs to the user's specification. This tends to be rather more expensive than the ready-made package. A thorough investigation of the market needs to be made before undertaking this step, as the likely outcome is a considerable increase in the cost of the overall exercise.

The final choice could be a half-way house approach of having the ready-made package tailored to your requirements. If the supplier is capable of making refinements to the standard package to suit the user's needs, then this could be the best solution.

Writing a Program

At one time it would have been unthinkable for the user to write his own programs. This was thought to be far too complex a business for the layman, and only highly qualified specialists were considered suitable for this task. Indeed, the early computers were difficult to program because of the primitive language techniques and their very limited memory capacities.

With the development of high-level languages, however, and the increasing sophistication of operating software, it is not too onerous a task writing simple one-off programs. Most people of average intellect should be able to cope with the problem. When it comes to designing whole systems, then it is probably time for a specialist to be called in. However, if the manager is required to calculate, for instance, the average weekly value of goods sold in a certain area over the last 12 months, then, assuming the computer held the necessary data, the program would consist of a simple formula of addition and division laid out in a logical fashion. This is analogous to how a clerk may be instructed to do the job with manual records, thus:

> START
>
> Read a sales record
>
> Does it relate to sales area X?
> (if not go back to START)

```
            Start
              │
              ▼
       ┌────────────┐
       │  Read a    │
       │  sales     │◄──────┐
       │  record    │       │
       └────────────┘       │
              │             │
              ▼             │
         ╱ Is it ╲    No    │
        ╱ dated within╲─────┤
        ╲ last 12    ╱      │
         ╲ months? ╱        │
              │ Yes         │
              ▼             │
           ╱ Is  ╲    No    │
          ╱ it the╲─────────┤
          ╲ last  ╱         │
           ╲record?╱        │
              │ Yes         │
              ▼             │
       ┌────────────┐       │
       │ Add sales  │       │
       │ value to   │       │
       │ total value│       │
       └────────────┘       │
              │             │
              ▼             │
          ╱ Is sales╲  No   │
          ╲ area = X?╱──────┘
              │ Yes
              ▼
       ┌────────────┐
       │ Divide total│
       │ value by   │
       │    52      │
       └────────────┘
              │
              ▼
       ┌────────────┐
       │Print average│
       │   weekly   │
       │   sales    │
       └────────────┘
              │
              ▼
            Stop
```

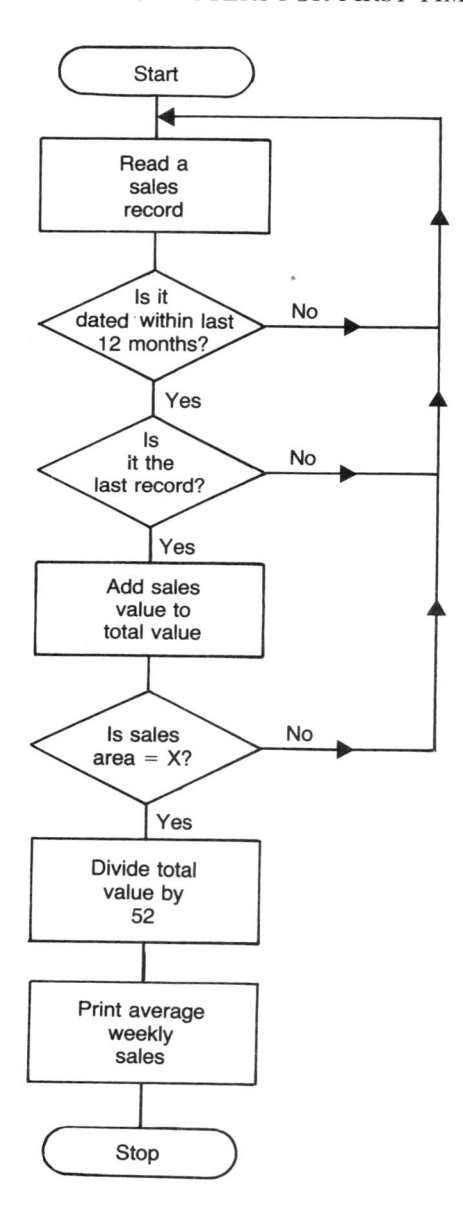

Figure 2.3   Program Flowchart

COMPUTER APPRECIATION

Is it dated within the last 12 months?
(if not go back to START)

Take the sales value and add it to a total value

Is it the last record?
(if not go back to START)

Divide the total value by 52

Report the answer

STOP

As can be seen from the above example, the computer can be programmed to switch from a serial sequence of instructions to another sequence. When the sales area indicator is X, it will have found the required sales area, and will continue with the next serial instruction. Any other result will cause the program to 'switch' or 'branch' to another instruction; in this case 'Go back to read a sales record'. This sequence of instructions and the branches can be set out in diagrammatic form in a 'flowchart' (Figure 2.3).

A TYPICAL INSTALLATION

Let us now pay an imaginary visit to a typical computer installation and see how such an installation is organised, and the sort of work which it is probably handling.

System for a Small Manufacturer

Let us take the example of a small manufacturer who is making engineering components for stock (Figure 2.4).

In the manual system, orders come in and a clerk has to price the order, check the customer's credit and send the order to the warehouse. If the goods are available the warehouse make out a packing note and despatch them. The packing note copy will come back to the office where in due course an invoice will be prepared and sent to the customer. If the goods are not available, the order will probably go on a file somewhere until another consignment has been manufactured.

The production manager will probably get copies of unfulfilled orders so that he can plan further production of those items. He should also be getting an analysis of regular demand so that he can maintain production

Figure 2.4 Manual System

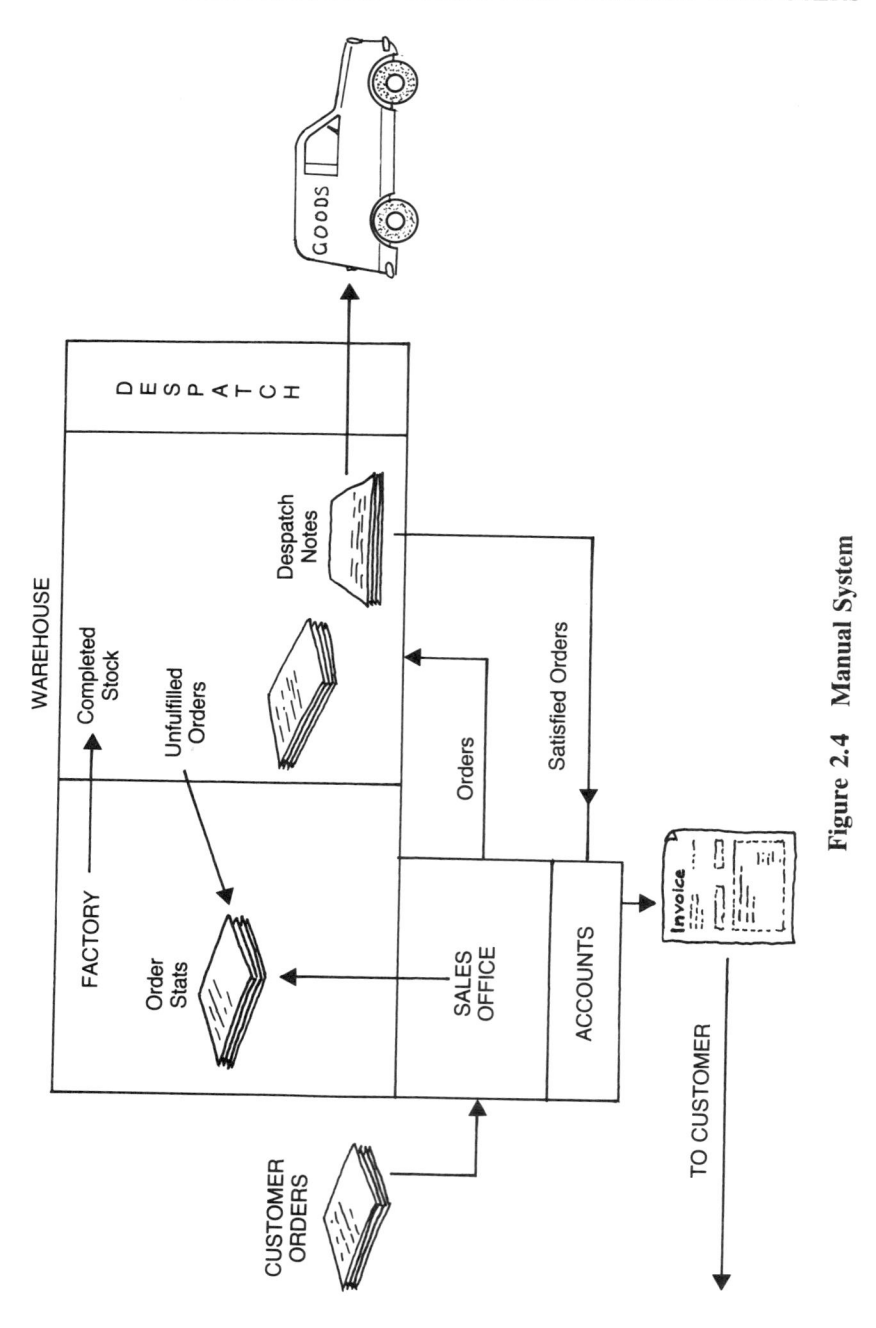

schedules and stocks. All invoices and other financial transaction details must be filed clerically to produce monthly statements, budgetary analyses and so on.

The Computer System

There are four main 'files' held on disks. Any sequence of records held on the computer is referred to as a file (Figure 2.5).

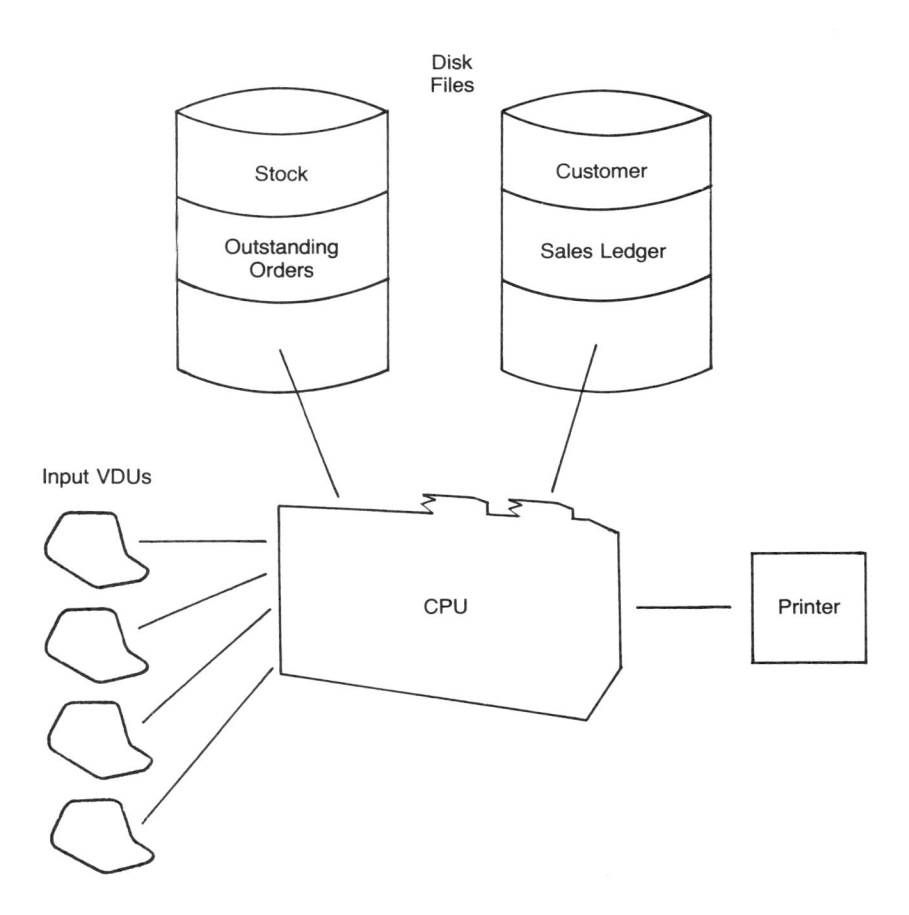

Figure 2.5 Computer Configuration

Customer File: This would consist of one record for each customer, each record containing: account number, customer name and address, credit rating, discount rate, and account balance.

Sales Ledger File: This would consist of one record for each customer, each record containing: invoice details, credits and cash receipts, and details of a customer.

Stock File: This would consist of one record for each stock item, each record holding: part number, description of part, stock location, price, quantity discounts, stock level, outstanding order quantity, mimimum stock level (eg calculated on 2 weeks moving average of orders), and re-order quantity (eg calculated on 6 weeks moving average of orders).

Outstanding Order File: This would consist of one record for each order item, each record containing: customer number, part number, quantity ordered outstanding.

There are two VDUs in the Sales Order Office. As orders come in by post and telephone, the operators key in the details to the VDU (Figure 2.6). The computer program checks the customer's credit and the availability of the stock (Figure 2.7). If it is a telephoned order, the customer can be told immediately if his order can be supplied. The quantity ordered is subtracted from the amount held in the stock record, and a despatch note is created which is recorded temporarily on a disk. Later in the day, these despatch notes are printed out and sent down to the warehouse.

Meanwhile, in the warehouse they key into another VDU new stock

COMPUTER APPRECIATION

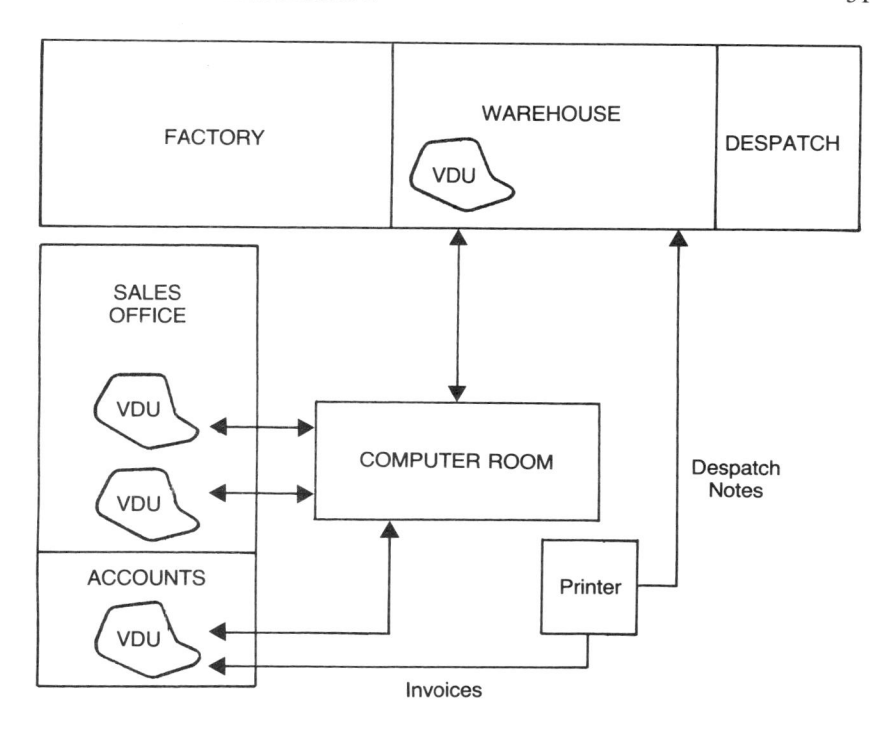

Figure 2.6 Computer Configuration – Physical Layout

received from the factory, plus any other changes to the stock position caused by returns, damaged stock and so on. All these go to update the computer's stock records, so that there is always an up-to-the-minute picture of the stock position held on the computer's files. At the end of the order processing run, the computer, from its recorded despatch note information and from the details of prices, discounts and so on held on the stock and customer files, can produce the relevant invoices for that day, and update the sales ledger with invoice totals (Figure 2.8). Any cash received from customers is also posted to the sales ledger file via a VDU in the accounts department, plus any other transactions to the customer or sales ledger files, such as credits, name and address changes, and so on.

At the end of each week, the stock file is processed by the computer to find which items have fallen below the minimum level. A list of those that

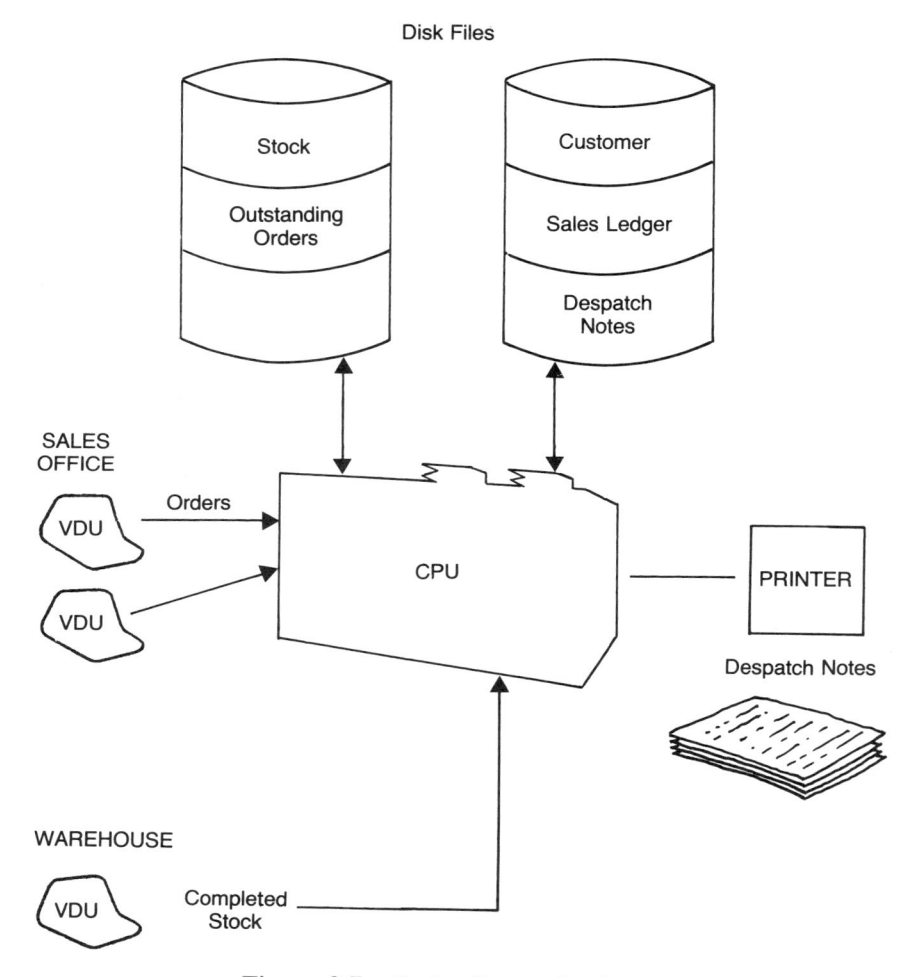

Figure 2.7 Order Processing Run

have is printed out showing the existing stock level, the re-order quantity, and the unfulfilled orders (Figure 2.9). The production manager can then use this as his schedule for planning the following week's work. If the necessary codes are stored on the stock file, the computer could produce a machine loading analysis, and a raw material requirements listing. The computer could control stocks of raw materials in the same way as it controls stocks of finished goods.

COMPUTER APPRECIATION

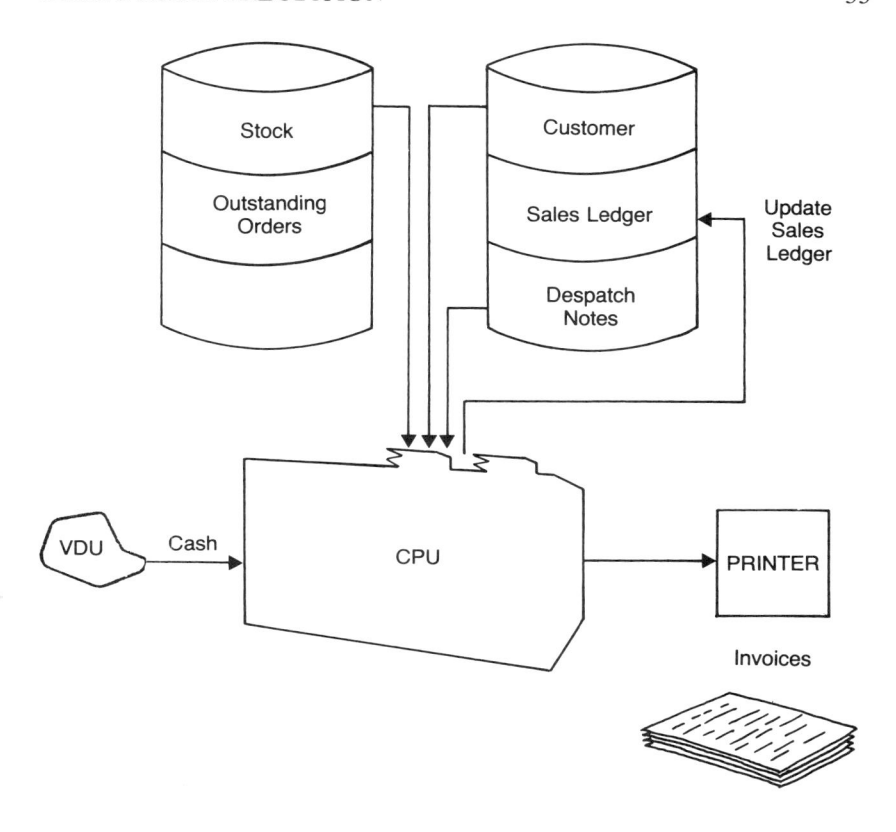

Figure 2.8 Invoicing Run

For raw materials and other purchases, a purchase ledger file could be set up, operating in much the same way as the sales ledger, with accounts staff keying in purchase invoice details, credits, and details of payments sent.

At the end of each month, the computer will send out customer statements from the sales ledger details which it holds on file, together with a master list of debtors, analysed by age of debt. If necessary, the computer could print out reminder letters (Figure 2.10). Similarly, on the purchase side, an analysis of the company's forward commitment can be

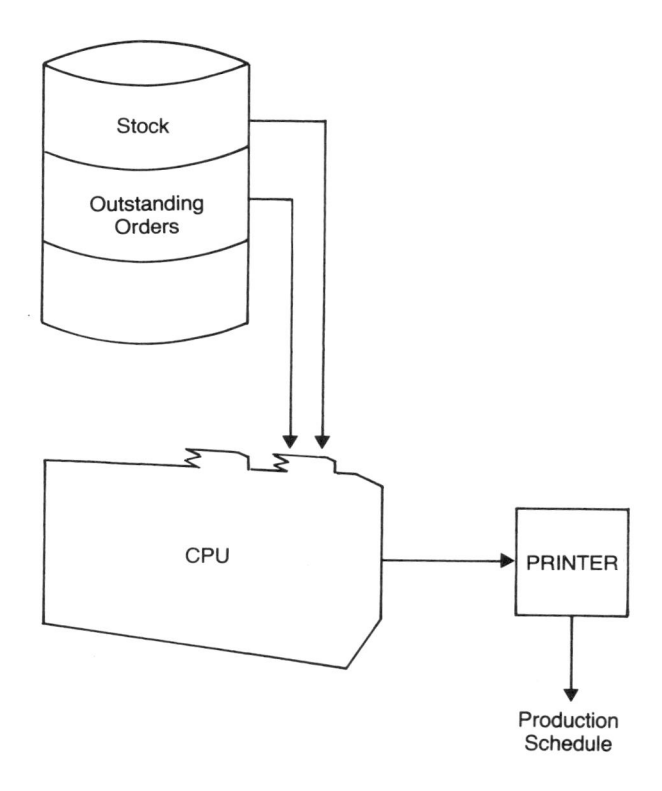

Figure 2.9 Weekly Production Schedule Run

printed out at the end of each month. If required, the computer could even print the company's cheques. At the end of each monthly period, the sales and purchase ledger details could be analysed against budget headings. The accounts department could key in other expenses not covered by the sales and purchase ledgers, to give a full profit and loss statement for the period. All these records could be accumulated over the financial year, so that at year-end the company's complete balance sheet could be printed out.

If the weekly payroll is an arduous clerical task, it could be performed on the computer with a weekly print of payslips and analysis reports.

COMPUTER APPRECIATION

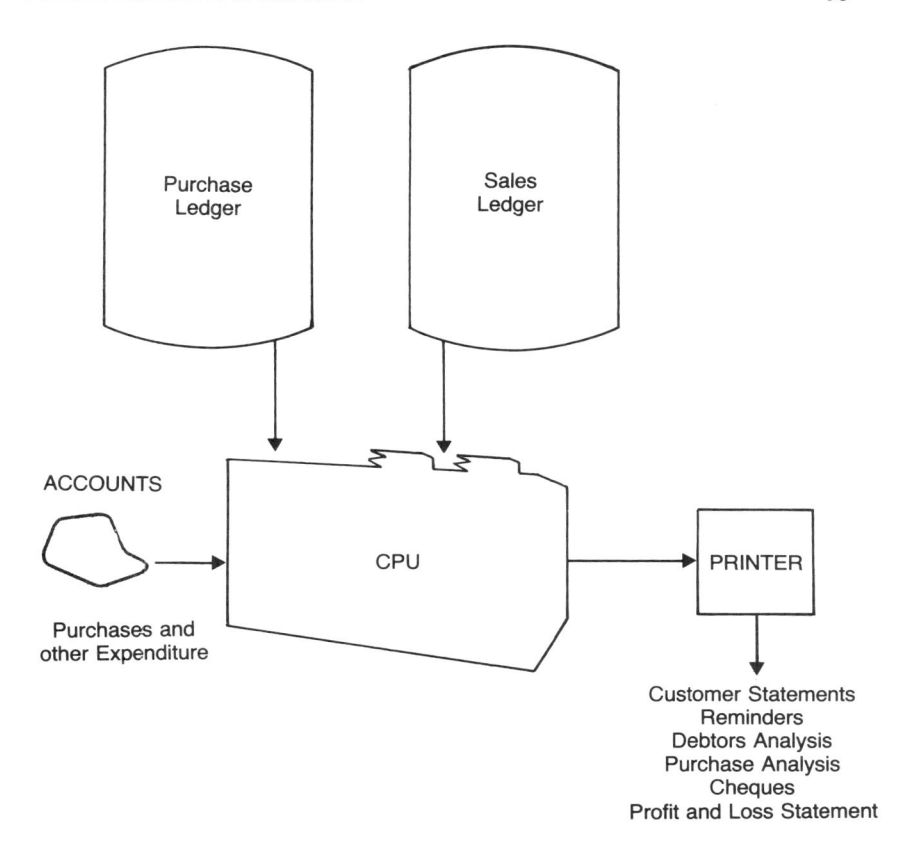

Figure 2.10 Monthly Sales and Purchase Ledger Runs

Relevant details from the payroll file could be transferred to the consolidated monthly accounts, along with the details from the sales and purchase ledgers.

When not being used for keying in transaction data, the VDUs could be used as enquiry terminals. Management would be able to obtain ad hoc information on individual customers, stock items or orders. For example, if a customer telephoned in to enquire the whereabouts of his order, information could be obtained for him in seconds.

So we build up a picture of the computer as the complete information centre of the company, with sales, accounts, and production department all keeping it posted with the latest transaction information, and all having easy access to that information via the VDUs situated conveniently in their own work places.

The Central Computer Function

In this function there will probably be an operations supervisor, responsible for the system as a whole, making sure that all the day's routines are completed successfully; that the disk file copies are maintained; that there are adequate stocks of paper, and other media; that the computer is always manned; and that the VDUs are functioning correctly. He will also be responsible for remedial action in the case of any failure of hardware or software; and he may also take on small programming and system maintenance jobs.

The operations supervisor will probably need at least one operator (who acts as his deputy) who at the beginning of the day will flick the appropriate switches on the operating console to power up the machine and to load the disks. From the operating console he will key in the first instruction to call in the operating software, which then takes over control of the machine.

The VDU operators will then be able to call in their programs, by keying in a simple instruction and the name of the programs, such as 'RUNSALES'. The central computer then probably requires little attention except when the operator has to load special stationery, eg for the despatch note, or invoicing run.

At the end of each day a summary of the day's runs, and perhaps a 'day-book' listing for audit purposes, showing details of all transactions, cash posted and invoices raised, will be printed. It is also customary to make security copies of the files held on disk. This can be quite easily done by loading a blank disk and copying to this from another disk, but this depends on their being two exchangeable disk units or 'drives'; otherwise copying can be a long and complicated procedure.

Security copies will normally be held outside the computer area in a special fire-proof safe, so that in the event of any disaster occurring the company's files would always be intact, and available for processing if necessary on another machine.

COMPUTER APPRECIATION

SUMMARY

The computer can be introduced into the average company's daily working life without disrupting routines, merely formalising them. The clerical staff lose the chores of heavy-volume typing, calculating and filing, and have their minor errors picked up by the computer at an early stage before they cause further trouble.

Management gain the advantage of regular information presented much earlier than previously; and customers benefit by a faster turn-around of orders and up-to-date information on stock availability.

It should be stressed that the computer will only be as efficient as those who are supplying it with data and interpreting its information. It is still the slave to its users, and will only act intelligently when given valid data and instructions to work upon.

3 The Feasibility Study

INTRODUCTION

This chapter covers the work involved in moving from initially considering a computer through to possibly preparing to go out to tender. The important word here is 'possibly' since the outcome of this stage could be a decision not to acquire a computer and so it is important not to prejudge the situation and assume that a computer is inevitable.

It is also important to remember that because the price of small business computers has fallen remarkably in the last few years, it is perhaps not as necessary to spend as much time on this phase of the selection procedure as has been the case in the past. These days, the justification for a computer is often the simple argument that extra staff will not have to be employed in the near future. At the bottom end of the minicomputer range, it is sufficient to be able to offset the cost of the computer against one member of staff. Because of this, some organisations find it difficult to justify undertaking a detailed feasibility study, especially in view of the time and effort involved. Thus, they assume that considering a computer is sufficient justification for acquiring one. This is obviously rarely the case. Any item of equipment should be justified both in its own right and especially in relation to other possible methods of achieving the same ends. A computer system should be no exception. This does not mean that every step outlined in this chapter must be rigidly followed, especially when the computer under consideration is less than £10,000. What is advocated is a selection approach to the chapter by choosing to carry out only those stages of the feasibility study which can be justified considering the overall price of the computer envisaged.

The work involved is in three essential stages. The first stage involves translating the initial thoughts about a computer into firm objectives and targets against which the computer and other options may be judged.

The second stage is the basic 'hard work' phase and involves identifying the particular areas of the organisation which are involved; examining these areas in some depth by documenting the associated procedures and assessing the relevant quantitative data involved; and finally, with reference to the objectives, deciding on the possible ways of achieving those objectives.

The third, and crucial stage, is concerned with taking all the documentary evidence collected in stage 2 and assessing, as far as possible, all the costs and benefits associated with each stated option. Using this assessment a decision can then be made as to which is the best course of action to take. This may or may not be to acquire a small computer system.

The feasibility study should examine the problems and possible solutions, and, if a computer system is justified, should also produce other important results. These will include the following:

— what tasks the computer should undertake;
— the volumes of work the computer should be capable of handling;
— the likely 'shape' and size of a suitable computer system;
— the magnitude of the likely costs involved, both acquisition and running costs;
— the other important 'side effects' which should be recognised, especially those on personnel and organisational procedures.

These outputs will be essential. They will ensure that not only is a computer justified but also that the particular nature of the computer system is appreciated. You will then be in a position to prepare a tender document knowing exactly what is required, and thus be able to dictate what you want and not be dictated to.

In brief, the feasibility study is an insurance policy; firstly against making the wrong overall decision, and secondly against getting the general idea right but the details wrong.

One of the problems with feasibility studies is that no two are the same. Each study varies both with the nature of the organisation concerned and

THE FEASIBILITY STUDY

also the particular problems and applications involved. For this reason it is impossible to be precise about every detailed step involved in such a study. However, to overcome this problem as far as possible and to attempt to give the flavour of the study, relevant practical examples are included where possible. These are reinforced by the last subsection, which gives a practical example of a feasibility study and implicitly suggests how the method and the results of the study should be presented in report form.

Because of the potential variability of individual studies, it is difficult to be definite about where specialist advice should be used. However, suggestions are made at appropriate points in this chapter, and these should be carefully noted and related to your own study once it is undertaken.

THE AIM OF THE STUDY

There are many and diverse reasons why you may have first started thinking about using a computer:

— your major competitors have bought a computer;

— your existing accounting machines are falling apart or receiving reduced or no maintenance support;

— a persistent computer salesman has persuaded the chief accountant to examine computer usage;

— difficulty in finding and keeping good clerical staff;

— your business is expanding at such a rate that you need more information to be able to manage properly;

— a long-established system is becoming overstretched;

— a specific problem such as new VAT or tax rules threatens to reduce accounting procedures to chaos;

— your service to customers is deteriorating;

— you never have enough of the right items in stock, but a lot of the wrong ones.

On first examination, some of these reasons may appear to be rather narrow and trivial, especially when one realises that they could result in an expenditure of many thousands of pounds on a system which could affect one's entire organisation.

It is therefore important to establish what you wish to achieve in terms of overall objectives and not rely only on the initial reason, although this may in itself justify some particular course of action. For example, although there may be overstocking in stores, this could well be a result of not monitoring changing demand, or over-ordering, or even uncontrolled production runs. The net result however could be to hold the wrong stock, or too much of the right stock. This in turn could result in deliveries to customers being delayed, or to cash flow problems. Thus defining the objectives to be improved – delivery performance or tighter control of cash flows – would implicitly encompass the stock control function.

Depending upon how information moves around your organisation, it will be clear whether a problem in a particular area affects other areas, or whether changes in one area will have wider effects. It is rarely the case that a particular department is totally self-contained in the data it needs to function and the information it produces as a result of its function. It is thus important to identify the flow of information around the organisation as this will then determine all the interconnected areas and thus all the applications that should be considered.

For example, the objectives of improving delivery performance could involve the following applications:

    Sales Order Processing

    Stock Recording and Control

    Purchasing

    Purchase Ledger

    Invoicing

    Sales Ledger

    Nominal Ledger

None of these areas can function satisfactorily without at least one of the others, and so to examine one implies potential examination of the others. Figure 3.1 shows how the various areas of an organisation may be linked by the information flow.

It will thus be necessary to look at your organisation in some depth, to identify the problems and where they occur, and define the overall

THE FEASIBILITY STUDY

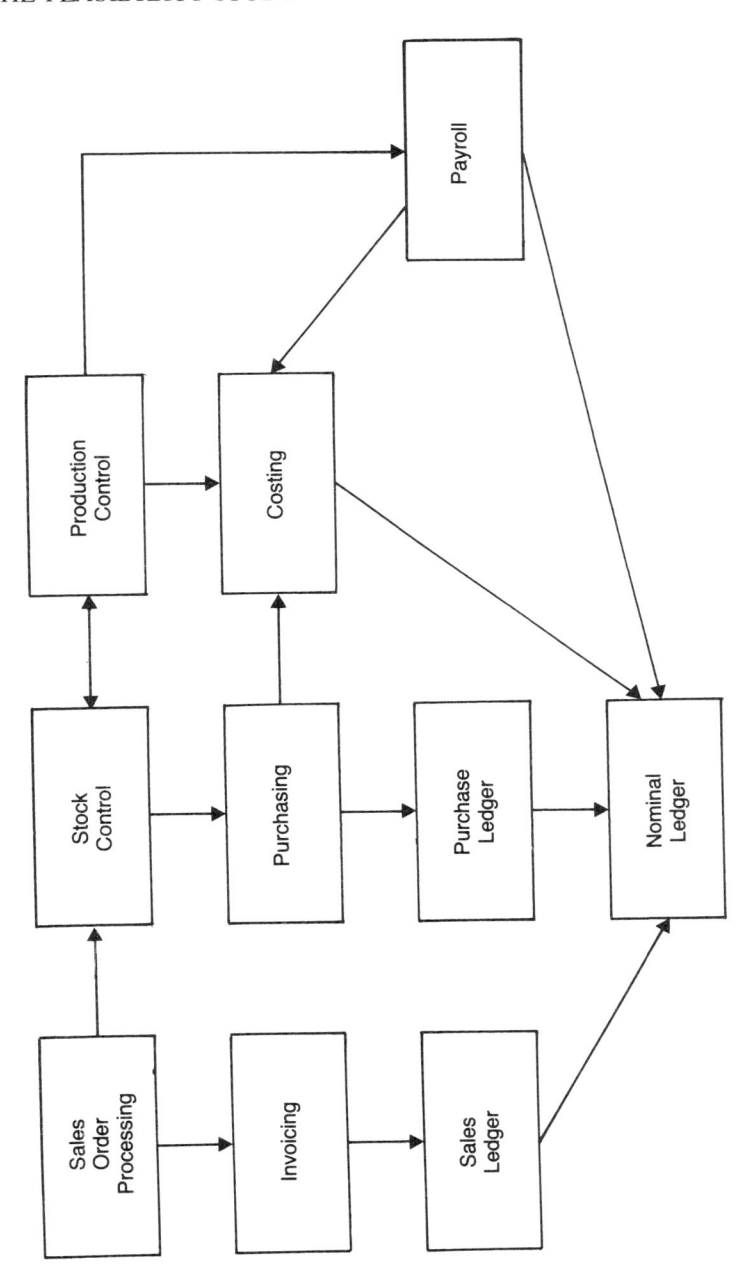

Figure 3.1 Example of Information Flow

objectives. By examining the information flow, the application areas to be studied can be identified.

Since this stage does not involve a computer, unless of course one is already used at some point in the organisation, it should be possible to undertake the work internally, as long as an objective approach is maintained.

RETAINING A CONSULTANT?

There may be occasions during the feasibility study, and perhaps more likely during the later stages of the computer acquisition process, where technical details are required or specialist assistance is needed. On these occasions you may be well advised to consider calling on a qualified consultant. Finding such a consultant can, however, be easier said than done. Consultants acting as advisers to companies considering the installation of their first computer come in all different shapes and sizes. Some of the best advice may come from your friends and colleagues, but this is unlikely to be comprehensive enough for your specific circumstances. Some good advice can be obtained from the computer manufacturers, but it is virtually impossible for the first-time computer user to distinguish between advice given sincerely by a manufacturer and sales arguments which it is his business to put to you.

Because small business computers are still relatively new, there is unfortunately little experience from which an independent consultant can draw when retained by a first-time user. Much of the best experience available is to be found among those consultants who may not be strictly impartial. It is equally unfortunate for the first-time computer user that there is no single and universal professional qualification that allows consultants to practise in the computer field.

It is therefore hardly surprising that in this twilight world not everything that goes under the heading of consultancy is impartial, independent and disinterested. Indeed some computer manufacturers' representatives carry visiting cards that label them as systems consultants – they are often authorities on their company's systems solution and perhaps those of their main competitors, but that is all. At least their visiting cards also show the name of the manufacturer they represent, which is not true of some of the middlemen of the industry. These may succeed in giving people the impression that they will give advice which is in the interest of the client, and proceed to do just that. Whether such advice is exclusively

THE FEASIBILITY STUDY

given in the interest of you, the client, is a completely different question. For although the opportunity for the payment of a commission to an 'independent' consultant is sometimes given, most of the advisors who have a vested interest in the selection of their clients' computer systems have made much more discreet arrangements. You should be aware of this even if you then decide that it is not a material factor and decide to retain this firm. Indeed the real cynics have it that their company's interest will ultimately be better served if the consultant retained has a vested interest in the project!

Those practising as consultants can be more accurately described by their original functions:

(i) Accountants

Large accountancy practices have been established in the computer consultancy field for many years. As a result they have developed probably the broadest base of experience of the evaluation and implementation of business computer systems, including those for the smaller firm. Their basic financial expertise has been extended to include most commercial systems. But their very size, and the scale of professional fees that reflect their expertise and standing, have made them seem remote to many smaller companies. It is fair to say that this source of advice represents a good, safe, practical approach to computerisation, and has the obvious advantage of the integrity of service that the profession's ethical code requires.

It is important to note that the previous remarks apply to 'large' accountancy practices. Almost without exception, small accountancy practices are not qualified to give any advice regarding computer acquisition, even though the systems to be computerised may be 'accounting' systems. Many small firms without a full-time internal accountant rely heavily on occasions on the advice given by their external accountant, but the installation of a computer should not be one of those occasions.

(ii) Management consultants

Much of what is said above regarding large accountancy practices can be said of the major established firms of management consultants, which also work to a similar ethical code. In general, however, many of these firms have specialised in highly technical assignments and as a result have great depth of technical expertise which may not be relevant to the situation of the first-time computer user. Unless a firm has a division specialising in consultancy work for the small business computer system, the services and fees of these large firms are not likely to be relevant to your situation.

(iii) Software houses

Software houses have plenty of practical experience. Their main function is the specification of systems and the programming of systems for their own customers and often on a subcontracting basis for the equipment suppliers. Either way they have business relations with a number of suppliers. The tooling-up costs that they face in running their businesses – computer time or rentals, recruitment and training of their skilled staff and the length of the learning curve that is inevitable each time they start work on a new piece of equipment – ensure that all but the very largest companies try to concentrate their efforts on a small number of manufacturers' equipment. Firms in this situation have a vested interest in the outcome of your selection decision, however hard they may try to keep the consultancy activities separate from the main business. At least one such firm offers a 'free' consultancy service and will provide a shortlist of possible suppliers to meet your systems requirements. The catch is that, having selected one of the suppliers nominated by the consultants, all the software work has to be done by the same firm.

(iv) Systems houses

Some systems houses have taken their experience of tailoring computer equipment and systems for their clients a stage further, and have developed packaged systems using the equipment that they have experience of, offering these systems directly to potential customers. Many of these firms still offer a consultancy service, even though the same firm has an agency agreement with an original equipment manufacturer. It is important that you are aware of any such arrangements that a consultancy firm may have made before they are retained. Unfortunately, you will probably only establish the facts by asking very direct questions.

(v) Academics

Many universities and business schools encourage their teaching staff to get their feet wet by taking on management consultancy. This can be a relatively economic way of buying pure intellectual skills, but in general such people have not had the opportunity to gain the essential practical experience of computerisation in the smaller company.

(vi) Independents

This category includes some of the best and some of the worst of all sources of advice. The 'unacceptable face' of consultancy is represented by those people who adopt this cloak purely to gain your confidence, before introducing the vultures who prey on whatever weakness your company shows. The disposal of the equipment that your first computer replaces is not, for example, normally considered to be part of a consultant's brief.

There is a small number of independent consultants who have built a reputation for integrity and quality of service, often specialising in a local area or a specific industry. If you are recommended to retain this type of consultant by a personal friend or business acquaintance you must be sure of the impartiality of the recommendation. Having done this, and established that the brief lies within the man's competence, this approach can often produce a very satisfactory relationship, with a high degree of involvement and personal commitment to the computerisation project, and at a reasonable cost.

(vii) Parent company internal staff

If you are a subsidiary company of a large group, you may be offered the services of an internal consultant. Whether this service will turn out to have been in the interest of the group or your own company will depend entirely on the parent company's policy in this situation, and perhaps on its politics. The advantages of this approach lie in the likelihood of the internal consultant having a head start in the understanding of your line of business and the reporting needs of the parent company if these form part of your systems requirements. Whether the internal consultant has the necessary experience of small business computer systems is another question. In some groups, the internal systems consultants have built up an excellent reputation for guidance without interference in their subsidiaries' computerisation activities. The acid test should still be whether the service offered is the most suitable for your company's circumstances.

You can choose to seek advice and assistance at any stage of the computer project. However, the normal brief is for one or more of the crucial stages of:

Establishing feasibility

Selecting a supplier

Implementing the system

Each of these assignments calls for different specialist skills. If you decide to retain one man or one small firm for all these stages you are asking for both breadth and depth of experience. You may think this is reasonable in exchange for fees billed at a daily charge rate of between £70 and £100. Yet however conscientiously a consultant may strive to further the client's interest, he is faced with the problem of keeping up-to-date in a very fast-moving industry. Many consultants can offer the breadth of experience that you may be looking for, but have decided to let others go first with the application of the newest developments. This attitude may often be in the client's best interests, but a consultant's natural caution should not be the reason for ignoring an attractive new development. The consultant is retained to advise you what risks associated with each type of approach are – not to decide on your behalf which approach to adopt.

Selection

Selecting a consultant is a dress rehearsal for selecting a computer supplier. The key is to shortlist a small number of firms with relevant experience; both the British Institute of Management and the Computer Services Association can help in this respect. Your auditors may be able to arrange to make introductions. You should allow the firms to comment on the desirability of handling only part of the assignment – supplier selection without a feasibility study, for instance.

Some firms may help in the selection process by offering a preliminary survey 'without obligation', which will help you to assess the firm's approach and give you the chance of seeing the calibre of their staff. Each firm's report should be evaluated in respect of:

— understanding of the aims of the assignment;
— definition of the service (advising vs doing);
— duration of the assignment;
— estimated cost and terms;
— methods and procedures;
— measurement of the success of the assignment.

There is no reason why you should not contact a firm's existing clients to develop an opinion of its suitability for your aims.

THE DETAILED STUDY

Preliminaries

The detailed study involves three sequential steps namely:

— investigate the application areas;
— identify the possible future courses of action;
— establish the costs, benefits and implications of each course.

Not until the second step does the computer rear its head, and even then the computer option may be one of two or three alternatives. Thus throughout this chapter there will be no assumption that a computer is inevitable.

It is important, before actually starting on the detailed study, to translate the application areas to be studied into the relevant departments and sections. This can be done by reference to the information flow and by noting where a particular function is undertaken. For example, all the ledgers may be handled by the accounts department, whereas sales order processing may involve sales department, credit control, and despatch. This identification will also permit the separate investigations to be undertaken in a logical fashion.

Investigation

The investigation involves collecting and collating all the facts about the various procedures used in a particular area. In doing this it is again useful to consider how the information flows, and to regard the procedure as an information processing system as described in Chapter 2. Thus, you should examine the Inputs, Processes, Outputs and Storage.

In looking at the inputs one needs to ascertain the following details:

— where does the information come from, ie another department, a supplier, a customer, etc?

— in what form does the information come, ie by telephone, letter, order form, supplier's invoice, etc?

— how much information comes in, eg how many times per day or per week, how much information each time?

— the actual nature of the information, eg if it is an order form what information is on the form?

The processing covers the use that is made of the input information, either some or all of it, ie what do you do with it? Do you copy it, change it, pass it on intact, ignore it, or use it to do something else?

The results of the processing will be to either generate outputs (which will probably be further information) or possibly to initiate an action such as a manufacturing process. As with input you need to collect particular details as follows:

— where do the outputs go?

— what form do they go in?

— how many outputs and how much information per output?

— the actual nature of the outputs.

There are many instances when the processing requires not only the inputs but also filed data to go with it. For example, a customer places an order, but before that order can be fully processed you may have to check his discount qualifications by reference to his account. This standard information kept in his account is therefore the stored data. Similarly an output may be to add to or change an item of stored data such as posting to a ledger or changing a stock item balance. You will therefore also need to collect certain data about these files of stored data, such as:

— what is the nature of the file?

— how many entries are there in the file?
— how much information is there in each entry?
— what information is in each entry?
— how often are entries accessed, changed and added to?

Wherever quantitative data is collected you should also try to estimate other related data. Firstly, if one is talking about the frequency of occurrences, such as new orders per week, then not only should you obtain the average value but also the likely maximum value. The maximum is necessary to establish the worst situation that has to be catered for with any future system.

Secondly, the data collected will refer to current values only. If you are to decide on a course of action to cater for the future then it should be able to cater for a number of years hence, say up to five. You should thus, where possible, obtain reasonable estimates of likely growth so that a percentage can be applied to the relevant figures to produce possible future values.

It is important, during the investigation, to identify and note any irregularities or variations from standard procedures, how complex are the procedures and how many separate procedures there are. For example, an order arrives for a non-standard product peculiar to a particular customer. What special procedures are involved? How many such cases are there? What extra information is required? What extra or different outputs are produced? Such cases will be of particular importance when you come to examine the possible option of using a computer in the future.

As an aid to the investigation a very brief series of questions and answers is given below. This relates to a very simple sales order processing application.

a) Inputs

How many orders per week?	– 200 av, 300 max
Are there seasonal variations?	– No
In what form do orders arrive?	– 80% standard form
	10% telephone
	10% letter
Do all orders come direct from the customer?	– Yes

How many lines per order? — 2 av, 5 max
What information is on an — Name, address and
   order?   customer order number.
   Item code, description and
   quantity
Are there any special procedures? — No

b) Processes
What actions result from — A five-part set is
   an order?   filled out
What information is on — Customer code numbers,
   date,
   this set?   item codes, item quantities,
   order number
Is any other data required — The customer code number
   that is not on the form?   (kept in filing cabinet)
What use is made of the — The customer credit is
   data on the order form?   checked. The item code
   and description are verified
What other actions are — The original is filed by
   taken?   customer

c) Outputs
What outputs are there? — The five-part set
Where do they go? — Part 1 – acknowledge-
   ment to customer
   Part 2 – Accounts
   Part 3 – Stores
   Part 4 – Despatch to
   accompany order
   Part 5 – Sales Office file

d) Storage
How many customers are there? — 200
How many products and groups? — 20 (1 group)
How many files are kept? — 2 – customer file
   – product file
What data is in the — Name, address, delivery
   customer file?   address, credit rating, dis-
   count

THE FEASIBILITY STUDY

What data is in the product file? — Product code and description

Many other questions would be required in a real situation but this may give some idea of the scope and detail required in an investigation. Appendix 1 gives some sample questionnaires for a number of standard application areas. These may be used as guides but you should note any other questions required to complete the investigations in your particular situation, especially those relating to variations, non-standard situations, etc.

It is very common for problems and difficulties to be caused by the sheer increase in workloads, or to be the result of gradual changes in the circumstances of an organisation. In such cases, the procedures have usually been changed, added to or modified slightly to cater for the evolving situation. This results in complex systems with many irregularities and quirks which can only be effectively operated by the member of staff who has been with the organisation for years and knows the system inside out. This person usually carries a large portion of the procedures in his head and cannot easily be replaced. When he has to be replaced, or when there is no such member of staff, a lot of time is spent in combating the system or 'fighting fires' rather than performing the routine operations. Thus the rationalisation of the procedures and systems could well be a prerequisite to other options.

To summarise, the investigation should generate the following information:

— the volumes of data involved, both average and maxima, and predictions of growth;
— the nature of the data;
— the complexities of the procedures and the irregularities;
— the relative timings of activities;
— any problems and shortcomings with the procedures.

Timings are important in cases where there is a need to improve lead times and a need to generate outputs on a particular day, such as payroll. The problems and shortcomings will come to light either by comment, or by deduction from the investigations. They should be carefully noted as they will point to particular facets of a procedure that should be corrected with a future system.

Identifying the Options

In the course of the investigation, as noted above, certain problems and potential problems may have come to light. These, the basic reasons and objectives behind the study and the information collected should now be used to assess how best to resolve the problems and achieve the objectives.

Since a computer system is one of the reasons for this study it is as well to consider how and why a computer can be useful. Satisfaction of some, or all, of the following criteria could suggest that a computer could be considered for the future:

— the existence of large volumes of input/output data;
— the repetitive nature of the processing;
— the logical complexity of the processing;
— the need to search and process large files of data;
— the need for very quick access to the data files;
— the use of large numbers of clerical staff;
— the mere existence of difficulties and problems;
— the need for better planning and control, and thus for better management information.

These criteria, and indeed similar ones, result from the basic advantages of a computer; namely that it can perform repetitive logical processing at extremely high speeds and store large volumes of data in a compact form. With reference to these capabilities possibly using specific criteria such as those above, you should be able to ascertain whether a computer could qualify, or whether it should actually be disregarded.

Even though a computer may qualify, it is unlikely that it is the only possibility. Other alternatives could be to increase staffing levels or to reorganise the existing systems and to attempt to bring them up-to-date. One option may actually be a combination, such as to rationalise and modernise the systems and procedures prior to introducing a computer system. This could appear to be unpalatable in view of the likely time-

THE FEASIBILITY STUDY

scales involved but such options should not be dismissed lightly, especially when one considers that:

— computer systems require rational and disciplined clerical systems surrounding them;

— computer systems are not introduced overnight in any situation; they take many months in practice;

— the costs involved will not be small and so a rushed decision should be avoided;

— it is the longer-term objectives which are the target.

The adoption of any alternative should also be related to organisation policies. For example, it may be that there is a definite policy to constrain staffing levels, in which case the option of a wholesale staff increase would be unacceptable.

It is with such considerations in mind that you should identify the various options. It could be argued that if a computer system is one of the options then you should be more specific and state, as far as possible, the broad nature of the computer system that should be considered, eg should it be an in-house computer or should you use a bureau? Such questions are better left to the next step when the consultant should be called in.

Evaluating the Options

The evaluation is easy in concept but difficult in practice. There are many facets to cost or evaluate, some of which will be unknown at this stage, whilst others are not susceptible to quantitative assessment, eg what is better information worth?

Costs fall into two broad categories:

— *capital costs,* ie the costs involved in implementing the chosen course of action;

— *operating costs,* ie the costs involved in operating the chosen course of action (marginal costs).

It is important not to underestimate capital costs. Development of new systems often takes longer than intended, and, unless fully understood, capital equipment can work out to be more than anticipated.

The benefits will also fall into two categories:

- *direct benefits:* staff savings, general overheads, reduction in overtime, reductions in stock, etc;
- *indirect benefits:* better information, improved morale, better customer service, etc.

For each option, one must set down a list of all the costs and all the benefits and then attempt to quantify them. For the options which concern a computer you should discuss the possibilities with the consultant, both in drawing up the list and allocating values to the items.

As an example of the cost involved in acquiring and running a small computer system, Appendix 2 gives a list of the possible capital and operating costs that should be considered. The importance of noting and assessing all these costs is evident when one considers that the basic acquisition cost of a computer system is only about half of the total expenditure that will be involved in running that system for five years, ie for a £30,000 system a further £30,000 could be involved in running the system over five years. However, before undertaking this exercise there is another problem that must be tackled, ie deciding on the nature of the computer system that is best suited to your requirements. Using the consultant, you should decide upon the type of computer system required, and its size. By the type of computer system, one is referring to questions such as:

- bureau or in-house machine?
- on-line or batch system?
- on-line update or on-line enquiry only?

It is impossible to indicate here how to answer these questions. Their resolution is entirely dependent on the particular situation in question. For example, the requirement for an on-line system may be dictated by the need to always have up-to-date information on current stocks available to the sales office because of the large numbers of new orders that arrive each day. Alternatively, it may prove impossible to decide between, say, using a bureau or acquiring an in-house system, and only when costs are considered will it be possible to make a choice.

An estimate of the overall size and the detailed configuration is essential for costing purposes alone. Once again the four elements of input, processing, output and storage should be considered in building up a picture of what is likely to be required.

THE FEASIBILITY STUDY 57

Using the data collected during the investigation and with the objectives in mind you should assess the requirements for each of the four elements with the consultant.

The following illustrations may be useful (note: this list is not exhaustive);

a) Processor Size
- batch or on-line system;
- the number of simultaneous tasks;
- the general complexity of the tasks.

b) Input Units
- the nature of the inputs;
- the frequency of input, eg orders per day;
- the volume of data per input, eg lines/order;
- the location of input staff, eg stores, sales office.

c) Output Units and Size
- the nature of the outputs, eg reports, invoices;
- the frequency of output, eg invoices/day;
- the volumes of output, eg lines per report;
- the location of required outputs.

d) Storage Size
- the number of data files, eg stock file;
- the volume of data per file;
- the number of transaction and history files;
- the efficiency of storage utilisation.

Factors such as these will be used to produce an estimate of the likely configuration of a computer system.

Having established the various possible courses of action, including the selected computer system, you must establish the costs and the benefits associated with each one. For any non-computer option this is an exercise which only you can undertake satisfactorily. This is because it will require business judgements and a knowledge of your organisation's operations which only you can provide. This also applies to some extent to the benefits that could accrue from a computer system, but reference to the objectives and discussions with the consultant should overcome any problems.

For the costs involved with a computer system then you should consult the consultant. He will be able to detail all the costs likely to be involved in your case and also put some projected values to these.

Once all the costs and benefits have been drawn up you should be in a position to analyse the results and start to make a decision.

ANALYSING THE RESULTS

With all the documentary evidence to hand you are now almost in a position to make a confident decision about which option to take up. However, there is one final set of factors which should be considered prior to making the decision. Whatever course of action is chosen it is likely to involve significant changes in the way in which your organisation functions. In other words it will have organisational and personal implications that must not be overlooked.

Due consideration must be given to these factors before the decision is made. Firstly, no matter which option is chosen, the involvement of senior management is of paramount importance if a successful conclusion is to be reached. This implies time and effort which must be devoted to the project, over and above normal day-to-day activities. In fact as any new systems or procedures are implemented, the time of more and more staff will be required to ensure smooth implementation.

Secondly, new systems and procedures can mean new offices, new job content and so on. The acceptability and effects of such factors must be allowed for.

For computer systems in particular there are some important points to note:

(i) the implementation of any computer system will involve clerical, and possibly shop floor, disciplines over and above those needed in a manual system.

THE FEASIBILITY STUDY

(ii) a tremendous amount of extra work will be involved in the implementation of a computer system; computer files will have to be created and verified, output checked, and new methods of working will have to be accepted.

(iii) although the employment of a person with specific computer expertise is not always necessary, it will be vital to allocate one person to be responsible for the overall computer system. This person should be able to dedicate the whole of his/her time to the project; implementing computer systems is not a part-time job.

He/she will have to liaise with management, the hardware supplier, the software supplier if there is a separate one, and any ancillary suppliers. The liaison will have to continue throughout the implementation and day-to-day running of the system.

In summary, the implementation of a computer system involves a great deal of work, involvement and willingness to cooperate by everyone concerned and should not be treated lightly. The 'press the button and it will appear' approach should be treated with a great deal of scepticism.

One further, but extremely crucial, factor is the acceptability of a computer system. Computers are often surrounded by myths and misunderstandings, which in turn can lead to distrust, and, in some cases, outright rejection of a computer system. It is therefore important to prepare for this, assess the possibility of it occurring, and plan to overcome it, if necessary, by a training and awareness programme.

Once these social and organisational factors have been identified and allowed for, then the decision can be made as to which course of action to take. This will involve looking at the costs and benefits, allowing for the other factors and selecting the best option. It is a decision only you can make.

If a computer system is chosen, the study should also have produced the details outlined in the introduction to this chapter and you should now be in a position to proceed with selecting your system.

THE STUDY REPORT

It is worthwhile, when undertaking the study, to document its progress so that the basic arguments for and against any particular option are clearly laid out. It may be that the decision will be made by a board or a similar group of managers. In such cases it is essential to present them with all the relevant data and arguments so that they are in a position of knowledge to make a decision.

To assist in this documentation an example of a study report is given in Appendix 3. It must be emphasised that the layout and contents are suggestions only and that any actual report will depend upon the particular organisation, the particular problems, the stated objectives, the possible options and so forth. These factors will determine the level of detail required in the report and the necessity to include any back-up data.

The report will also serve as a formal record of why any solution was selected, what were the objectives it was to meet, and what were the potential costs and benefits. It may thus be possible to use it as a yardstick against which to measure future progress.

4 Going Out To Tender

INTRODUCTION

If, as a result of the Feasibility Study, the viability of computerisation is agreed, the next stage is to prepare a tender document upon which suppliers can base their proposals. The format and content of this tender document is described in Appendix 4.

A list of four to six suppliers should then be agreed and the tender document sent to each supplier with a covering letter. A specimen of the covering letter is included in Appendix 5. The date by which suppliers' proposals should be available should be within four to six weeks of the date they receive the report. During this time period the suppliers may possibly contact the company for clarification of certain points contained in the tender document. However, the tender document in itself should be comprehensive enough for the suppliers to prepare their proposals without the need for collecting any additional facts from the company.

THE TENDER DOCUMENT

The purpose of the tender document is to give the prospective suppliers an insight into the size of the company and its expected growth rate, its type of business and the applications to be computerised. The tender document should also guide the prospective suppliers as to the format and content of their proposals.

The tender document itself will take the form of a report entitled 'Specification of Computing Requirements' and the following subsections describe its content. Reference should be made to Appendix 4 which contains a specimen report.

Introduction

The introduction to the report explains why a computer system is being sought and gives a brief outline of the company: type of business, location, current turnover and expected growth rate, etc. The introduction describes the overall format of the report and explains what type of solution is required.

Generally, for the first-time user of computing, the type of solution required is one which provides both the equipment and all the programs necessary to run the required applications. This type of solution is often termed the 'turnkey' approach and means that all development and testing of the programs is the responsibility of the supplier. If this type of solution is required this fact should be pointed out in the introduction.

Adopting the 'turnkey' approach may mean that more than one supplier is to be involved in providing the complete system. This is because some manufacturers of equipment do not themselves maintain the staff for the development testing and implementation of the programs to run the required applications. This is particularly true when programs have to be tailor-written rather than using off-the-shelf programs (often termed applications packages) which can often be utilised with maybe some minor tailoring for standard applications. If more than one supplier is to be involved, the introduction to the report should acknowledge this fact but point out that ideally only one contract is to be placed and that the leading organisation should ideally take responsibility for the system as a whole.

Computer Applications

This subsection of the report describes the requirements of each of the applications proposed for computerisation. Reference should be made to the Appendices of the report which show details of volumes, frequencies and files.

Mention should be made of the proposed implementation plan, showing the preferred order in which the applications are to be computerised. This ensures that if a particular application is to be implemented initially as a stand-alone system it should be designed to accept manual input, and if this application subsequently interfaces with another computerised application it should perhaps have the facility to accept computer-generated input.

GOING OUT TO TENDER

Any applications which it is considered may possibly be computerised within the next 5 years, but are not to be included in the suppliers' original quotation, should be mentioned here. These must however be identified as possible enhancements to the system.

The requirements of each application for which the supplier is required to quote should be described. Any specific requirements regarding the locality of input, enquiry or output terminals should be defined; for example, the requirement for a terminal to be dedicated to telephone sales even though from the input volumes it may appear that one terminal is sufficient to service all orders.

Suppliers' Proposals

This subsection of the report is included as a guide to be used by the suppliers when they are preparing their proposals. It identifies a number of section headings which the suppliers are requested to adhere to when formatting their proposals, in an attempt to standardise the layout of the proposal documents. The details to be contained in each section are also identified so that each supplier should submit information on the same topics.

Section 3 of the specimen tender document should be referred to. This itemises the details the supplier is required to submit.

Appendices

The prime purpose of the appendices is to specify the volume of transactions for each application. Ideally, an indication of the item details maintained on each record within each file should also be given, showing where possible the number of characters in each item. No attempt should be made to design the layout of the computer files, but a guide to record content and the number of characters in each item presents a useful guide for suppliers to estimate computer file storage requirements.

Appendix A4.3 of the Specimen Tender Document shows an example of the format of a Sales Ledger Record. The items within the record are listed and alongside each item is given an indication of the number of characters within each item. As an example, the numbers of characters within the Customer Account Number is shown as 9(8). The 8 in brackets represents the length of the item, ie 8 characters, and the '9' prefix indicates that the item is numeric. The 'X' prefix used for the Name and

Address item indicates that the item is alpha/numeric. An 'A' prefix can be used to indicate that a field is alphabetic. The record and file size are estimated, having made the point as an introduction to the Appendices that no allowance has been made for any file indexes or any blocking of data. (With some manufacturers complete records must be packed into a fixed length area called a block.)

In addition to showing the volume of transactions and a guide to record content for each application, an outline of the requirements of each application should ideally be included. This outline of requirements should show Inputs, Files, Processing and Outputs. An example of such an outline for a Sales Ledger/Sales Analysis application is shown in Appendix A4.1 of the Specimen Tender Document. The frequency of production of any output documents should be shown on the outline of requirements and their size should be apparent from the volume figures.

SELECTING A LIST OF SUPPLIERS

Having completed, in as much detail as possible, the Specification of Computing Requirements Report, it is suggested that a short time be spent with a qualified consultant to check through the content of the report, answer any outstanding queries and agree a list of prospective suppliers.

Guidance should be sought from the consultant in agreeing on the list of suppliers. Some of the questions which should be asked are : Can the supplier provide a suitable system within the company's budget? Is local hardware and software support available? Does the supplier have any experience in any application areas specific to the company? Has any contact already been made between the company and any supplier? What, if any, equipment is already used by the company? All these factors should be reviewed by the consultant and the company to derive a list of four to six suitable suppliers. However, if this task is to be performed on your own, then perhaps a few remarks on what small business computer suppliers actually supply are in order.

When you buy a small business computer from an established manufacturer, typically over 50 per cent of the purchase price is 'thin air' – the supplier's operating costs of marketing, sales promotion, sales commissions, salaries and bonuses, recruiting and training, software development and maintenance, field engineering support, and the company's overheads, profits, and the big intangible cost of customer support.

GOING OUT TO TENDER

If all suppliers had identical products, identical costs of sale, identical operating costs and profits, and were equally established and competent, then any variation in price between their products would be a direct measure of the level of support provided to their customers. Even though this is a hypothetical situation, the analysis does hold good at the extremes; a high level of support to a supplier's customers is never reflected in cheap prices, and conversely a supplier which pitches its prices substantially below the general market level will not be able to provide much support to its customers.

But between these extremes the analysis does not hold. Not only are there substantial differences between all the suppliers, but the situation is constantly changing. As the relative strengths and weaknesses of each supplier are in a constant state of flux, each supplier is forced to constantly review its business policy and terms. At any one time any or all of the following tactics may be pursued by different suppliers:

— preferential terms for customers ordering new equipment;

— penal terms for customers not ordering new equipment;

— 'end-of-line' special offers;

— sales promotion and commission premiums for end-of-line products;

— sales promotion and commission premiums for new products;

— cash settlement discounts;

— other special terms.

Many of these policies are 'gimmicky', and quite a few are self-liquidating offers. The supplier can be at least as well off, even without an increase in the volume of business, but the customer may not be aware that the special terms he has negotiated are illusory. It is always possible to shop around and find a marginally improved offer, but it is more important to be aware that there is flexibility in the situation and that this can affect you in different ways, some of which are of greater long-term benefit than an initial price reduction.

The cost of customer service and support is reflected in the level of resources and the budget that the supplier's line managers deploy. However hard some suppliers strive to provide a uniform level of service to all customers, the world just is not like that and the individual branch manager has to decide between the conflicting and various claims on his limited resources. Invariably, some customers get a much better level of service than others. This may all seem obvious, but it is still relevant when you consider that some other customer's problems can affect the delivery of your computer, the quality of your software, the response to your engineering call, the level of cooperation that you receive or even the price you pay for your computer.

Suppliers like to have a satisfied customer base, as much use is made of customer references in the selling of a computer system. But there is a conspiracy of silence that surrounds the dissatisfied customers and this means that a supplier does not need to support its customers at any cost. When a customer is dissatisfied and the supplier believes that its obligations have been discharged, there are very few sanctions that the user can apply. Most suppliers will put in extra effort to try and recoup a bad situation, but if their recommendations are not followed they will often withdraw all but the minimum level of contracted support and retire to cut their losses.

Some suppliers have taken advantage of this predicament and pushed for quick, ill-considered orders, even though they know that these customers are only going to have perhaps a 50 per cent chance of achieving a successful computer installation, whereas the customers of the more responsible suppliers may have an 85 per cent chance. This trend is exaggerated by the fact that the more responsible supplier is likely to put more effort into winning the order from a company that shows an above average chance of becoming a successful customer reference; whereas the same supplier may decline to tender if it does not reckon your chances of being a success are high enough.

Computer suppliers have an unreasonably strong hold over their customers (a fairly common view is 'the customer is always wrong'). Yet some suppliers' customers get a high level of service and support, while others do not. Nearly every first-time user needs lots of support, and often more than has actually been contracted for.

Getting the Best out of Your Supplier

To make sure that you have the best chance of ending up in this privileged (high level of service and support) group you will need to adopt an approach which follows this pattern:

GOING OUT TO TENDER

(i) Respect

If your business is a personal success story, you have a head start, as any supplier is eager to be associated with this type of success. Respecting a supplier will represent no problem if it, too, has a successful track record, but you may find it more difficult to respect some of the young men who represent them. In fact, many young computer salesmen have acquired a great breadth of experience and business maturity very quickly. The salesman should have the all-important communications skills that enable him to talk to you and his company's technicians. If the salesman you are dealing with does not measure up on these counts, you may be talking to the wrong supplier; see if his manager comes out of the same mould.

(ii) Personal involvement

Any supplier will take you more seriously as a customer if it knows that senior management is fully aware of the importance of its involvement with the computer project. If it is clear that you have taken the trouble to find out what is going to be required at each stage of the project, and that you intend to remain in the driving seat until successful implementation of the system, then the supplier knows that you mean business. On the other side, staff turnover among suppliers is still very high, and your involvement should be with all those responsible for your well-being as a customer, and not any one individual.

(iii) Realistic plans

There was a time when computer manufacturers had a vested interest in encouraging customers to make unrealistic and over-ambitious plans. Nowadays most suppliers have a vested interest in judging just how realistic your objectives are and what level of complexity you are competent to handle. Suppliers will therefore respond more positively to the company that has specified its needs in detail for the few areas that are really essential to its business, than to the company that wants to do some of everything.

(iv) Professional approach

For suppliers there is little agreement as to what constitutes a professional approach. To some it means the ability to close orders quickly and abandon the customer to his own devices. To most, however, it means a fairly formal, structured method of working and the adoption of and adherence to standards. If you adopt this approach in your dealings with suppliers – written requests for information; regular, minuted progress meetings; the retention of a consultant; a written invitation to tender; the adoption of agreed standards and procedures – you show that you intend to remain in control of the project and intend to achieve a successful computer system.

(v) Customer reference potential

The threat of bad press is not much of a sanction if things have gone wrong in the relationship with your supplier. However any genuine plus points that you can offer – household name, introductions in your area or line of business, any newsworthy angles – can sometimes help to secure better support from your supplier.

5 Evaluating the Proposals

INTRODUCTION

Upon receipt of the suppliers' proposals they are to be evaluated. A demonstration of the hardware and where possible the software which each supplier is intending to propose is recommended at this stage. The recommended evaluation method is the use of the Weighted Ranking by Levels technique.

Having identified the supplier who best fulfils the requirements at an acceptable price, a contract is to be negotiated, the implementation plan formalised and the system implemented. These stages are all covered in Chapter 6.

The objectives of the evaluation are basically to ensure that the proposed systems can do the job and to select the best and most cost-effective solution to the company's data processing requirements.

It is possible that an actual review of the costs quoted in each of the proposals may immediately eliminate one or more of the proposals from any more detailed evaluation, simply because the costs quoted are outside the company's budget or the costs are well in excess of the other proposals. However, having eliminated these proposals it is necessary to review in detail the remaining proposals.

Once again, the same comment as was made in Chapter 3 applies here. The technique outlined in this chapter is an attempt to objectify the evaluation procedure, and should really only be attempted in conjunction with a qualified advisor. Failing this, or if it is felt that the system cost does not justify such a detailed technique, then a more subjective approach to the problem could be made by simply selecting from the features listed in the following pages a subset which is considered absolutely necessary, and measuring each supplier's proposal against this standard. This will certainly take less time, but it should be borne in mind that such an approach is open to all sorts of bias and external influences.

EVALUATION OF COSTS

All details of cost should be extracted from each proposal. It is suggested that costs are calculated over a five year time span and itemised for each supplier under the following headings:

Hardware

Maintenance

Applications Packages

Tailor-Written Programs

Any Annual Licence Fee for Software

Any Other Costs (eg training, installation, delivery)

Some suppliers charge a rental fee for Application Packages, others make a one-off charge. Some suppliers charge a licence fee for using their Applications Packages and Operating Software.

It is suggested that the costs extracted are exclusive of VAT and insurance and an example of a Cost Summary Chart is shown in Figure 5.1.

ANALYSIS OF SYSTEM FEATURES

The next task is to extract from the proposals, and subsequently evaluate, the facilities offered in each supplier's system.

Section 3 of the Specification of Computing Requirements report indicated to the suppliers the features of their system which are to be described. For evaluation purposes each of these features is to be considered. It is suggested that the 'Weighted Ranking by Levels' technique (Figure 5.2) is used to assist in the evaluation of these features. The technique involves assigning a weighting factor to each feature to reflect its relative importance. The weighting factor is based on the requirements for the system, the costs and organisational conditions.

When using this technique, the first task is to make a list of the feat-

EVALUATING THE PROPOSALS

Costs

Over 5 years – exclusive of VAT and Insurance

	Supplier A	Supplier B	Supplier C	Supplier D	Supplier E
Hardware	£20,519	£22,187	£17,095	£19,665	£25,500
Maintenance	£10,340	£11,120	£8,640	£9,825	£12,750
Application Packages	£4,500	£4,750	£4,250	£12,000	£6,000
Tailor-Written Programs	£8,000	£8,000	£9,000	–	£8,500
Licence Fee for Software	£1,967	–	£2,100	£3,750	–
TOTAL	£45,326	£46,057	£41,085	£45,230	£52,750

Figure 5.1 Cost Summary Chart

Specification Summary

Sheet 1
Weight 3.6
Prepared by:

Topic: HARDWARE

Questions: CPU SPEED

SUPPLIER A	0.5 μsec	8	28.8
SUPPLIER B	0.7 μsec	6	21.6
SUPPLIER C	2.2 μsec	3	10.8
SUPPLIER D	0.8 μsec	5	18.0
SUPPLIER E	0.6 μsec	7	25.2

Figure 5.2   Weighted Ranking by Levels

ures. This list should be compiled as follows. Firstly, decide on a major grouping of the features. It is suggested that four major groups are used: Hardware, Software, Support and General. Each group should then be further subdivided to give a lower level of detail. It is possible that a further subdivision will be necessary to arrive at the detail level which equates to the actual feature which is to be evaluated. An example of this grouping structure is shown in Figure 5.3 where the features to be evaluated from the proposals relating to the specimen Tender Document are listed.

It can be seen that the resulting list is structured hierarchically. Taking the Hardware grouping as an example its structure is as shown in Figure 5.4.

ALLOCATION OF WEIGHTS

Having completed a hierarchically structured list, the next task is to assign weights to each level. The weights are expressed as a percentage and they reflect the relative importance assigned to each element in a group. All the percentage weights for each level within a group should add up to 100.

EVALUATING THE PROPOSALS

Evaluation Table

EVALUATION TABLE – WEIGHTED RANKING BY LEVELS SCORES

LEVEL	ELEMENT	WEIGHTS 1	WEIGHTS 2	WEIGHTS 3	ACTUAL WEIGHT	WEIGHTED SCORES SUPPLIER A	SUPPLIER B	SUPPLIER C	SUPPLIER D	SUPPLIER E
1	HARDWARE	30								
2	CPU		30							
3	Speed			40	3.6	28.8	21.6	10.8	18.0	25.2
3	Size			60	5.4	43.2	43.2	5.4	43.2	43.2
2	DISKS		30							
3	Access Time			25	2.25	11.25	11.25	15.75	13.5	18.0
3	Capacity			40	3.6	28.8	21.6	18.0	21.6	25.2
3	Flexibility			35	3.15	25.2	25.2	25.2	25.2	25.2
2	INPUT		10							
3	Terminal Characteristics			50	1.5	12.0	12.0	12.0	12.0	12.0
3	Screen Size			50	1.5	12.0	12.0	12.0	12.0	12.0
2	OUTPUT		10							
3	Speed			40	1.2	9.6	9.6	9.6	8.4	9.6
3	Printer Width			40	1.2	9.6	9.6	9.6	9.6	9.6
3	Character Set			20	0.6	3.0	4.2	3.6	3.6	3.6
2	EXPANSION		20		6.0	36.0	48.0	6.0	36.0	48.0
	TOTAL HARDWARE SCORE	45				219.45	218.25	127.95	203.1	231.6
1	SOFTWARE	45								
2	Systems		30							
3	Operating System			60	8.1	64.8	64.8	16.2	64.8	64.8
3	Programming Languages			25	3.375	27.0	23.625	27.0	27.0	27.0
3	Utilities			15	2.025	16.2	16.2	16.2	6.075	4.05
2	APPLICATIONS		70							
3	Sales Order Processing			35	11.025	88.2	88.2	88.2	33.075	88.2
3	Sales Invoicing			5	1.575	12.6	12.6	12.6	7.875	6.3
3	Stock Recording & Control			35	11.025	88.2	88.2	88.2	66.150	88.2
3	Sales Ledger & Sales Analyses			5	1.575	12.6	9.45	9.45	9.45	6

Figure 5.3 (continued over)

Evaluation Table (contd)

EVALUATION TABLE – WEIGHTED RANKING BY LEVELS SCORES

LEVEL	ELEMENT	WEIGHTS 1	WEIGHTS 2	WEIGHTS 3	ACTUAL WEIGHT	WEIGHTED SCORES SUPPLIER A	SUPPLIER B	SUPPLIER C	SUPPLIER D	SUPPLIER E
3	Purchase Order Monitoring			5	1.575	12.6	12.6	12.6	12.6	9.45
3	Purchase Ledger & Purchase Analyses			5	1.575	12.6	12.6	12.6	12.6	9.45
3	Nominal Ledger			5	1.575	12.6	12.6	12.6	12.6	9.45
3	Payroll			5	1.575	9.45	12.6	12.6	12.6	9.45
	TOTAL SOFTWARE SCORE	15				356.85	353.475	308.25	264.825	322.650
1	SUPPORT	15								
2	Training		20		3.0	24.0	24.0	24.0	3.0	18.0
2	Maintenance		35		5.25	42.0	42.0	42.0	42.0	42.0
2	Systems Support		35		5.25	42.0	42.0	42.0	42.0	31.5
2	Back-up		10		1.5	12.0	12.0	12.0	10.5	10.5
	TOTAL SUPPORT SCORE					120.0	120.0	120.0	97.5	102.0
1	GENERAL	10								
2	Installation Requirements		15		1.5	12.0	12.0	12.0	12.0	12.0
2	Documentation		5		0.5	4.0	4.0	4.0	4.0	4.0
2	Implementation Plan		30		3.0	24.0	24.0	12.0	12.0	24.0
2	Delivery		10		1.0	8.0	8.0	8.0	8.0	8.0
2	Working Relationships with Supplier		30		3.0	24.0	24.0	12.0	12.0	12.0
2	Market Position of Supplier		10		1.0	8.0	8.0	8.0	8.0	8.0
	TOTAL GENERAL SCORE					80.0	80.0	56.0	56.0	68.0
	GRAND TOTAL SCORE					776.3	771.725	612.2	621.425	724.25
	POINTS/£1000					17.13	16.76	14.90	13.74	13.73

Figure 5.3 (continued)

EVALUATING THE PROPOSALS

The evaluation table (Figure 5.3) shows an example of the weights which were applied to reflect the relative importance of the features to be evaluated from the proposals relating to the specimen Tender Document (see Appendix 4).

This evaluation table at the level 1 assigned percentage weights of:

30 to Hardware

45 to Software

15 to Support

10 to General

These reflect the percentage importance of each of these categories to the ABC Company.

Each lower level is assigned weights in a similar manner so that an actual weight to apply to each feature can be derived.

As an example of how to calculate the actual weight, the CPU speed and size will be used from the evaluation table in Figure 5.3.

Level	Element	Weights			Actual Weight
		1	2	3	
1	Hardware	30			
2	CPU		30		
3	Speed			40	3.6
3	Size			60	5.4

Firstly, the weight for CPU is calculated as a percentage of the weight for Hardware, ie 30% of 30 equals 9. Then the weight for speed is taken as a percentage of the figure just calculated, ie 40% of 9 equals 3.6. Similarly, the weight for size is taken as a percentage of 9, ie 60% of 9 equals 5.4.

This procedure is followed for all features until all the actual weights have been calculated.

EXTRACTION OF SYSTEM FEATURES FROM THE PROPOSALS

The next task is to extract from each proposal details of the features offered by each supplier. As an aid to documenting this procedure it is

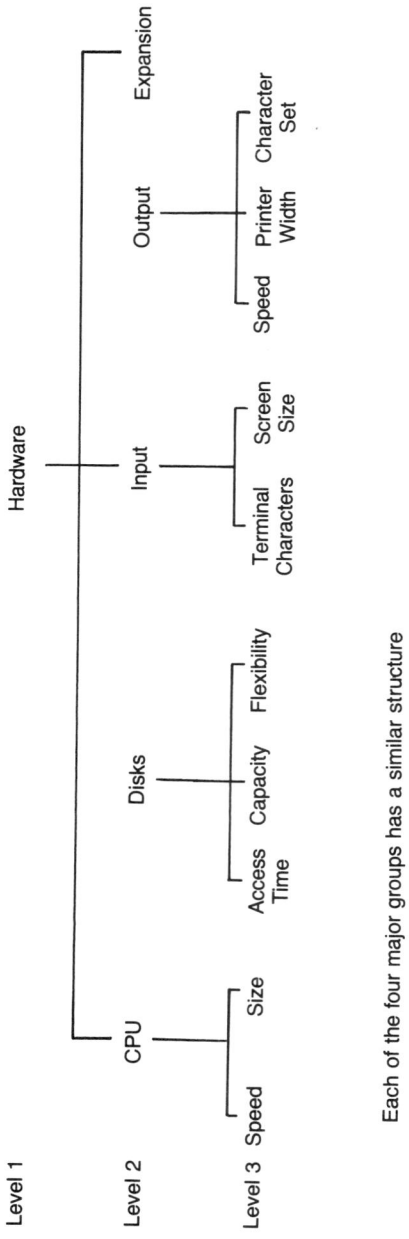

76 SMALL BUSINESS COMPUTERS FOR FIRST-TIME USERS

```
Level 1                        Hardware
                                   |
          ┌────────────┬───────────┼───────────┬───────────┐
Level 2  CPU          Disks       Input       Output    Expansion
          |            |            |            |
       ┌──┴──┐   ┌─────┼─────┐   ┌──┴──┐   ┌─────┼─────┐
Level 3 Speed Size  Access Capacity Flexibility Terminal Screen  Speed Printer Character
                    Time                        Characters Size         Width    Set
```

Each of the four major groups has a similar structure

Figure 5.4

EVALUATING THE PROPOSALS 77

suggested that an Evaluation Sheet is made out for each feature to be evaluated showing which feature it refers to, the actual weight to apply and the names of the suppliers whose proposals are to be evaluated (Figure 5.2).

The suppliers should have adhered to Section 3 of the Specification of Computing Requirements report (see Appendix 4) and presented all features as requested in a standard layout.

The details of the operating characteristics of the hardware will probably be included in the suppliers' proposals as fact sheets relating to each piece of equipment.

Examples of the type of features to be evaluated are given in the following list. It is divided into four parts:

Hardware

Software – systems and application

Support

General

Hardware

CPU Speed	The speed at which the processor performs its operations (eg to perform one addition, or to retrieve/insert data from memory).
CPU Size	The size of the processor.
Disk Access Time	The average time to locate data on the disk storage.
Disk Capacity	The amount of disk storage proposed.
Disk Flexibility	Whether exchangeable disk drives are proposed, making security copying easier.
Terminal Characteristics	The number of terminals proposed. The type of keyboard (eg separate numeric pad, etc). Removability of keyboard. Scroll or page facilities ⎫ specifically for Cursor facilities ⎭ VDUs.
Screen Size	Number of characters displayable on a VDU. Physical size.

78 SMALL BUSINESS COMPUTERS FOR FIRST-TIME USERS

Output Speed	The number of characters/second or lines per minute printed.
Printer Width	The number of characters printed per line.
Character Set	The number of characters available for printing. Upper and lower case available?
Expansion	The upgrading facilities on the machine proposed (CPU size, number of terminals, disk capacity, etc) and the upwards compatibility of the machine within the supplier's range.

Software

Systems Software

Operating System — The facilities offered by the operating system:

— ability to run more than one program at one time
— ability to support more than one VDU.

Programming Languages — The language to be used for the program development and the availability of other languages on the machine.

Utilities — The inclusion of any report generator/screen enquiry programs and software development aids which are simple for the user to write. Also the features of the sort and file-copy utilities.

Application Software

Hardware Constraints — Limits on size of application catered for:

— number of transactions
— number of customers, etc.

Are these limits dependent on:

— size of the CPU?
— type of file storage medium?
— the number of file storage units?

Maximum number of VDUs that can be supported.

EVALUATING THE PROPOSALS   79

Reliability   Is the application software reliable and easily maintained? This can only be ascertained by looking up the supplier's user references and asking such questions as:

— How easy to install?
— How satisfied is the user now?
— Any problems?
— Installed on time?
— How responsive was supplier to meeting your needs?
— Is documentation thorough?
— Was training adequate?
— What would you change?
— Is it efficient and reliable?

Flexibility   Can the application software be adapted to your requirements? For example are there user defined parameters available for:

— setting accounting periods in a general ledger?
— choosing either open-item or balance forward in a sales ledger?

If such parameters do not exist then either your application must change to suit the package or else the package will require tailoring, which can be very expensive.

Performance   Does the package perform as claimed? The only way to determine this (apart from asking other users) is to see a demonstration. Make sure, however, that the demonstration is on the same type and size of machine as that proposed.

Supplier Assessment   This assessment is almost a by-product of the time spent questioning the supplier's user references. However there are a number of other indicators:

— Well established and successful business? (see Annual Report, etc)

- Is supplier willing to guarantee performance and delivery in the contract?
- What post-delivery program maintenance is provided?

Portability — Can the application software be transferred to a different computer without modifications? It is perhaps only important that this compatibility should be available when the system is either up-graded with additional hardware or else replaced by another machine in the same range and from the same supplier.

Terminal Dialogue — The following factors should be taken into consideration when assessing the VDU screen formats and dialogue:

- Is it easy to use?
- Can it be operated by a casual rather than a dedicated user?
- Does the computer lead the dialogue, ie does it prompt for responses?
- Is there a menu selection capability?
- Form filling facility?
- Is the response time adequate?
- Is there uniformity between packages from the same supplier?
- Are there easy correction procedures for typing mistakes?
- Do the operator instructions stand out?
- Is it easy for the operator to ask for help instructions from the computer?
- Is the dialogue designed to minimise human errors?
- Is the dialogue designed to trap as many errors as possible immediately?

Documentation — It is important that the documentation provided should be available for inspection prior to the order being placed. Such documentation should include as a minimum, a machine operations manual describing the operating system and the

EVALUATING THE PROPOSALS

computer plus an applications installation and operating manual containing details on how to set up the packages (ie how to create and expand data files, etc).

Technical Support

In evaluating the technical support provided, the following questions should be asked:

— are training courses provided?
— how much support is provided for installation of the package?
— how long from date of purchase is technical support provided?
— if enhancements are added, does the purchaser receive updates? If so, is there any additional cost?
— any plans for such enhancements or alterations to the packages?
— is an error reporting service provided? If so, how?
— how many staff are available to support the package?
— where are the support staff located?

Support

Training

The range of training courses available, their venue – whether in-house training is available and how much does it cost?

Maintenance

The locality of engineering support:

— call out time
— time spent on preventative maintenance.

System Support

The responsibility for systems implementation:

— who is responsible?
— is it chargeable, etc?

Back-Up

The procedure in the event of machine failure:

— locality of similar machines
— battery back-up in the event of power failure, etc.

General

Installation Requirements	The necessity for any special environmental conditions: — air-cooling system — voltage regulator, etc.
Documentation	The availability of systems and programming documentation.
Implementation Plan	The acceptability of the proposed plan for systems design/programming/installation.
Delivery	The lead-time on delivery of the hardware.

SCORING OF SYSTEM FEATURES

Having extracted all details from the proposals and entered them on the evaluation sheets the next task is to allocate a relative score to each feature. It is suggested that features are scored out of a possible maximum of 10 points and the following table should be used as a guide to the scoring system:

 0 No value; does not exist
 1 Extremely bad
 2 Bad
 3 Weak
 4 Below average
 5 Average
 6 Above average
 7 Good
 8 Very good
 9 Superior; excellent
10 Perfect; cannot be improved

The score for each feature of each supplier's proposal should then be entered on the evaluation sheet and multiplied by its actual weight to give a weighted score. These weighted scores can then be entered on the Evaluation Table, as shown in Figure 5.3 and the weighted scores for each supplier summed up for each group (for example Hardware, Software, Support and General) and finally a grand total weighted score for each supplier should be calculated. This then reflects the technical merit of each proposal.

EVALUATING THE PROPOSALS

SELECTION OF THE BEST SOLUTION

Having extracted the total cost of each proposed system and derived a total weighted score for the performance of each system, the cost performance ratio can be derived. This ratio is shown in Figure 5.3 as a points/£1,000 figure. This is derived by applying the following equation to each supplier's figures:

$$\text{points/£1,000} = \frac{\text{grand total weighted score} \times 1000}{\text{total cost over 5 years}}$$

Having applied this formula to each of the suppliers' details, the supplier with the highest points/£1,000 ratio should be the one selected. The situation could arise when several suppliers have the highest ratios which are identical or are so close that making a decision from the information available is difficult. These proposals should be reviewed to determine in which areas each scored well or badly and the supplier should be approached to clarify the areas where scores were low. Unsuccessful suppliers should be thanked for submitting their proposals and told that it will be pursued no further. From discussions with the remaining suppliers it should be possible to identify the supplier who is offering the system best suited to the company's requirements. The other suppliers should be notified and the contract negotiated with the selected supplier. This and the following procedures are described in Chapter 6.

It is suggested that advice is sought from a qualified consultant regarding the allocation of weights and the scoring of the features. These tasks could be performed in a relatively short time span (one day for instance) providing that you have, as far as possible, extracted all the details from the proposals and entered them on the Cost Summary and the evaluation sheets. Further advice may be required if selection from a shortlist is to be performed.

THE EVALUATION REPORT

Introduction

It may be necessary for a report to be produced to outline the evaluation procedure and the considerations made in selecting a particular supplier. This section describes the format and content of such a report.

A summary sheet should preface the report explaining why any suppliers' proposals were rejected as a result of a preliminary evaluation. It should also state which suppliers' proposals were evaluated in detail and which supplier proposed the most suitable solution for the company. The report itself should then comprise the following sections:

1. Introduction To Report
2. Proposals
3. Selection procedure
4. Summary of findings
5. Conclusions
   Appendices
   Evaluation Table
   Cost Summary

The content of these sections is described in the following paragraphs.

Introduction to Report

This section explains that the report presents the results of an evaluation of the alternative proposals for the computer processing of certain applications. A list of the proposed applications should be given. It explains that the proposals were in response to a statement of data processing requirements prepared with guidance from a suitably qualified consultant. It briefly describes the format of the tender document in that it provided general outlines of the system to be considered and included information on volumes and file characteristics. In addition it points out that the suppliers were asked to supply information in their proposals to specified headings, so that, as far as possible, comparable information could be obtained from each supplier.

Proposals

This section gives details of when the tender document was sent out and to whom. The names of any suppliers whose proposals were rejected as a result of a preliminary review should be given along with the reason for the elimination from the detailed evaluation.

A selection is included giving a brief summary of each supplier's proposal which was considered in the detailed evaluation. Each summary should list the proposed computer hardware giving the following information:

— model number and size of CPU;

— disk capacity;

EVALUATING THE PROPOSALS

- number of data entry/enquiry terminals;
- number and speed of printer terminals.

Each summary should also give an overview of the proposed software; where applications packages are to be used or where tailor-written software is proposed.

Each summary should include the overall cost of hardware and the cost of software.

Selection Procedure

It is suggested that this section is subdivided into the following subsections:

General

This simply names the personnel who were involved in the evaluation.

Analysis Procedure

This explains that the procedure took the form of an analysis of the proposals received from the suppliers and that a list of factors relevant to the decision was drawn up (reference should be made to the Evaluation Table in the Appendices where the actual factors used are listed).

It should explain that these factors included an assessment of machine capacity and software and also covered items such as packages and the level of support and maintenance provided by the supplier.

It should explain that the various factors were grouped together under the headings Hardware, Software, Support and General and that each factor was then assigned a weight in relation to the importance to the company. It should then explain that the proposals were given a score for each of the factors; the scores were adjusted in relation to the weights and, as a result, an overall score was arrived at for each supplier's proposal. It should be pointed out that this procedure provided a rational method of combining together the many objective and subjective elements involved in making a decision.

Results of the Analysis

This summarises for each supplier, the overall score, the costs over 5 years and the price/performance ratio (reference should be made to the

Evaluation Table in the appendices where an analysis of the actual scores is shown).

It identifies the supplier with the best price/performance ratio. Should more than one supplier have price/performance ratios which are so close as to make selection of the best impossible from the information extracted from the proposals, a summary of the steps taken in choosing the selected supplier from these should be included.

Summary of Findings

This reviews for each supplier the main features of their proposal. It should highlight in which areas they scored particularly well or badly, explaining the reasons why.

Conclusions

This sums up the reasons why the selected supplier was chosen in preference to the others.

Appendices

This section contains an evaluation table (an example of which is shown in Figure 5.3) and a cost summary (an example of which is shown in Figure 5.1).

6 Implementation

INTRODUCTION

When evaluating the various computer systems available, the customer should have asked for a contract specimen to be supplied with each proposal. This will have been superficially examined prior to making a decision on the intending supplier.

Before committing themselves to that supplier, however, it is essential that the customer examine the contract in detail. In this chapter the main points to be watched for in a typical supplier's contract are reviewed and some typical contract contents are listed.

Having agreed the contract with the selected supplier, the next task is to plan for the implementation of the computer system. The computer will probably have been selected with certain limits as to costs and time laid down for its implementation. These may be critical to the profitability of the exercise; and at least, can cause considerable worry or embarrassment if not met.

Computer projects, like any other type of project, will not necessarily go according to plan; but it will assist the efficient management of the project if some plans are drawn up. The later sections of this chapter give an overview of a proposed implementation plan and also give a checklist of items which usually need to be considered in any computer implementation plan. (There may be other items in any individual project; or some items may be ignored.)

No manager needs to be told that time is money; and the implementation period of any computer system while the site is being prepared, systems tested, staff trained and so on, is an essential but unproductive time which needs to be properly controlled.

If things are getting badly behind schedule, the temptation is to cut corners. Questions get asked like: 'Do we really need another test?' and 'Can't staff complete their training after the system tests?'.

Such temptations can be very much more expensive in the long run, however; if errors are found or mistakes made after the implementation period they can be much more difficult to rectify. The only solution is to plan as thoroughly as possible at the outset, and to allow adequate time for everything that needs to be done.

CONTRACT OPTIONS

Assuming that the customer wishes to procure both hardware and programs there are a number of contract options to be considered:

> A single contract with the computer manufacturer to supply both hardware and programs.
>
> A single contract with the computer manufacturer to supply hardware and programs, the manufacturer subcontracting to a software house for the programs.
>
> A single contract with the software house to supply programs and obtain manufacturers' hardware for resale to the customer.
>
> Two separate contracts: one with a manufacturer for hardware and the other with a software house for programs.

It will usually be in the customer's interests to tie up both hardware and software in one contract, unless there are very good economic or technical reasons for doing otherwise.

SOFTWARE PACKAGE CONTRACTS

Points to watch out for:

> Is there a full definition of the package, describing user methods and procedures?
>
> Is there any warranty with the package?
>
> Will the package be installed for you?
>
> Are you permitted a trial period before acceptance?
>
> Is there any maintenance support with the package, and for how long?

IMPLEMENTATION

Are statutory changes to the package, such as those resulting from government legislation, issued free of charge?

Should a revised version of the package be released, is this offered, and if so at any additional cost?

What limitations are there on your rights to use the package?

Can its facilities be offered to a third party?

Can it be run on a bureau or another user's machine, in the event of breakdown?

Can the proprietor terminate your licence, or change the regulations controlling use of the package?

Are you allowed to make your own modifications or enhancements to the package?

Are source and object codes available to the user?

What happens to proprietorship of the software if the supplier fails?

SYSTEMS DEVELOPMENT CONTRACTS

Are the duties of supplier and customer well defined?

What are the terms regarding price and payments?

Is the supplier committed to completing the development by a certain date, and are there any penalties for failing to complete on time?

(Customers should be warned that this could backfire against them if adequate testing and maintenance guarantees are not secured.)

What are the relative responsibilities of supplier and customer for testing the programs?

What does maintenance of the software cover?

Is there any charge for program faults found after the acceptance tests?

What charges are there for amendments made at the customer's request? Is there a free maintenance period, and what does it cover? Is there a continuing charged maintenance service?

How will the programs be delivered? What documentation is supplied with them? When are they considered to have been accepted?

Does the customer have absolute ownership; and if not what restrictions are there as to use?

HARDWARE CONTRACTS

Is there a clear definition of the hardware covered by the contract, describing its capabilities?

Does the customer have any redress should the supplier's skill and judgement as to the suitability of the hardware prove defective?

Does the hardware price cover site preparation, delivery charges, installation and testing? Are any ancillary services such as supply of disk packs and operator training included?

When does hardware responsibility pass from supplier to user, and are there any additional insurance charges involved?

Is the price fixed, or is there any protection against arbitrary price increases?

What guarantees are there for the hardware's reliability during and after the implementation period?

Are the delivery dates firm?

Is there any protection against late delivery, or can the customer defer delivery if need be?

What maintenance service is offered; what are the charges; and what guarantees are there for continuing support should the hardware become obsolete?

Are there any restrictions on trading-in or upgrading the equipment?

TYPICAL CONTRACT CONTENTS

1 Definitions

This section is sometimes included to assign meanings to certain expressions used throughout the contract.

2 The System Specification

The supplier should agree to submit a detailed Specification of

Requirements report and give a guide to its content. The supplier should agree to amendments to this report providing they are received within a stated time period and providing the amendments fall within the scope of the system and the price originally quoted. The supplier will probably state that the Specification of Requirements report is the document which defines the extent of his obligation to fulfil the customer's requirements.

3 The Hardware

The supplier should agree to deliver and assemble the hardware on or near the delivery date(s) stated in the quotation at the stated cost. The supplier may demand exception from this agreement if delivery is delayed owing to any causes beyond the supplier's control.

Upon delivery the supplier may contract to subject the hardware to certain acceptance tests and demand signature of an acceptance document within a fixed time period. A subsequent warranty period may be provided. Any rules relating to the use of the hardware by a third party should be stated.

4 The Software

The supplier may contract for the customer to provide the necessary test data to facilitate acceptance tests on the software. Upon acceptance a warranty period may be provided. Any copyrights relating to the software and associated documentation will be itemised.

5 Management of the Project

The supplier should specify the policy regarding the allocation of a project team, supplier's changes in staff, provision of working accommodation at customer's premises for supplier's staff, availability and cost of supplier's personnel post-implementation – but during the currency of the contract.

6 Costs and Changes

The supplier will state here the action to be taken in the event of non-payment or termination of contract. The maintenance charges stated in the quotation may only be guaranteed for a fixed time period. If this is the case it should be stated in the contract. The supplier will most likely plead exemption from carrying the cost of any statutory price increases which are beyond the supplier's control. Should the prices quoted be exclusive of any additional costs, such as Value Added Tax, this fact should be shown.

7   Risk and Title

Here the supplier will probably disclaim all responsibility for loss or damage to either hardware or software once it is delivered to the customer's premises. When the title of the hardware and software actually becomes that of the customer should be stated. The effect on the contract of using the equipment in combination with other equipment not provided by the supplier should be stated.

8   Termination

The rules governing termination of contract should be itemised.

9   Maintenance

The terms of the maintenance agreement both preventative and remedial should be stated.

10 Communication

Whenever data is to be transmitted using a telecommunications link the supplier will probably ask the customer to provide any agreement required by British Telecom (BT) regarding the connection of Data Communications Equipment to the equipment belonging to BT. Any data transmission speeds quoted would remain the responsibility of BT, and similarly should BT require the supplier to make any modifications to the hardware, having previously approved the same, the supplier will probably state that this cost must be borne by the customer.

STAGES OF THE IMPLEMENTATION PLAN

Appoint Computer/Project Manager

When the computer has been selected, many organisations may feel that they can then rely on the supplier to design systems, install the computer, and generally organise everything related to the computer system.

Indeed, many systems suppliers will take on a great deal of this work for the client, but the ultimate responsibility for successful implementation will always rest with the client himself.

For this reason it is important that one of the client's employees at a

IMPLEMENTATION

fairly senior level be given responsibility for liaison with the supplier and for ensuring that things go according to plan.

If the client is employing a full-time computer manager to run the installation, he should be appointed at an early stage and can take on some of the responsibility for managing the project: but it is essential that he has director-level backing.

Ideally, therefore, a senior director of the client company should take on project management responsibility.

Prepare Implementation Plan

The appointed project manager should begin to liaise with the suppliers by preparing, with them, an implementation plan.

In its simplest form this can merely be a checklist of activities to be performed, although, as can be seen from Figure 6.1, many of these will be interdependent, and can be expressed as a network.

It is important that the client's project manager makes contact with the supplier at the appropriate level. Although the regular contact man may be the supplier's systems analyst, he may not have control over other resources, such as programming, hardware, etc.

The client therefore must seek out a senior manager from the supplier to advise on the implementation plan, and get the supplier to commit his forward resources to a definite schedule.

Agree Responsibilities for Activities within Implementation Plan with Suppliers, etc

Having agreed an implementation plan, the question 'Who does What?' must be asked. This might be a case of pencilling in names of responsible people against the individual activities in the plan.

The outcome of not doing so could be either duplication of effort, where two people are trying to do the same thing unbeknown to one another; or worse, things not being done at all.

When all the activities have been assigned, then some kind of reporting structure should be set up so that the project manager can ensure that everyone is carrying out their assignments. Regular progress meetings are generally the most convenient way of receiving reports from those

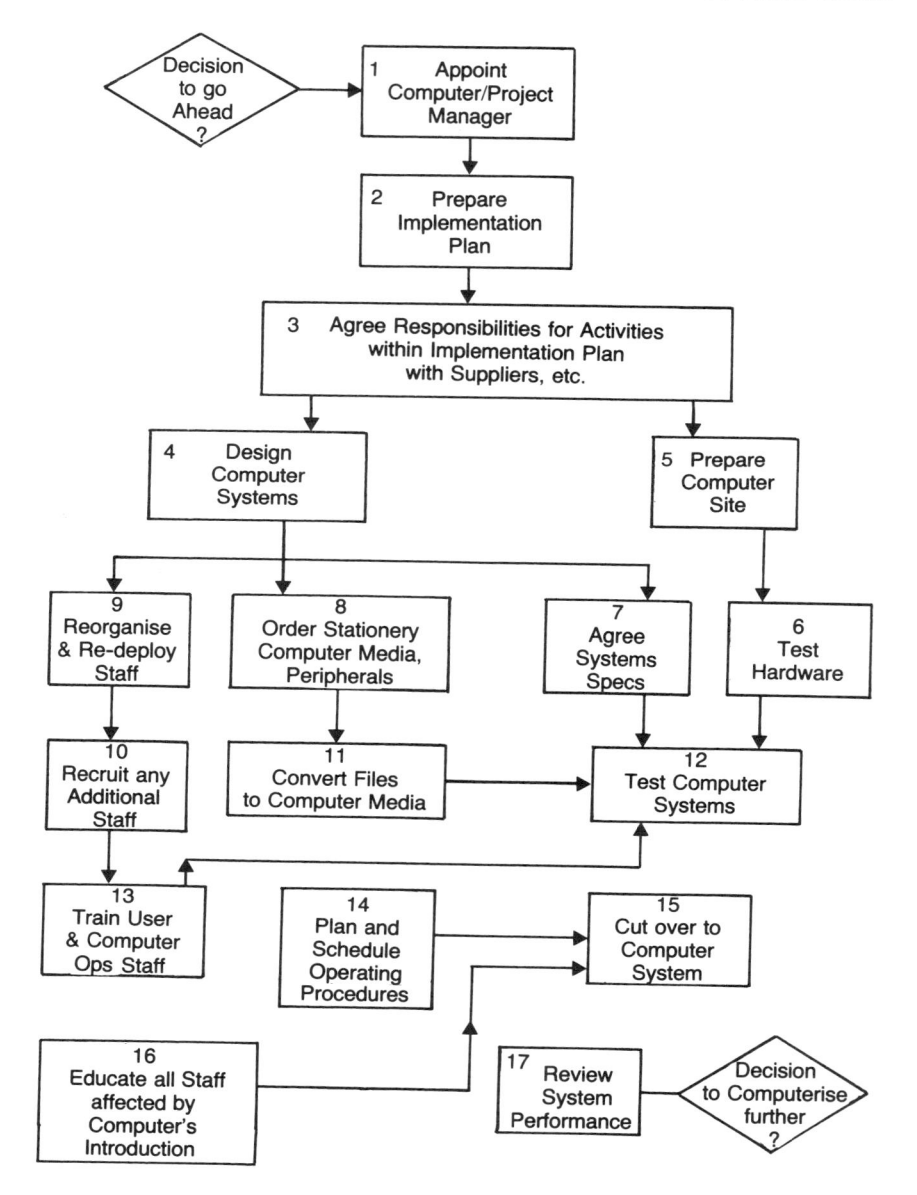

```
                    ┌─ Decision ─┐      ┌─ 1  Appoint ──────┐
                    │   to go    │─────▶│  Computer/Project │
                    │   Ahead ?  │      │      Manager      │
                    └────────────┘      └─────────┬─────────┘
                                                  ▼
                                        ┌─ 2  Prepare ──────┐
                                        │  Implementation   │
                                        │       Plan        │
                                        └─────────┬─────────┘
                                                  ▼
                          ┌─ 3  Agree Responsibilities for Activities ─┐
                          │         within Implementation Plan         │
                          │           with Suppliers, etc.             │
                          └────────┬──────────────────────┬────────────┘
                                   ▼                      ▼
                        ┌─ 4  Design ───┐       ┌─ 5  Prepare ──┐
                        │   Computer    │       │   Computer    │
                        │   Systems     │       │     Site      │
                        └───┬───────┬───┘       └───────┬───────┘
          ┌─────────┬───────┘       └────┐              │
          ▼         ▼                    ▼              ▼
     ┌─ 9 ─────┐ ┌─ 8  Order ────┐  ┌─ 7  Agree ┐ ┌─ 6  Test ─┐
     │Reorganise│ │  Stationery  │  │  Systems  │ │ Hardware  │
     │& Re-deploy│ │Computer Media,│ │   Specs   │ │           │
     │  Staff  │ │  Peripherals  │  │           │ │           │
     └────┬────┘ └───────┬───────┘  └─────┬─────┘ └─────┬─────┘
          ▼              ▼                │             │
     ┌─ 10 ────┐   ┌─ 11 ──────────┐      │             │
     │Recruit any│  │ Convert Files │─────▶┌─ 12 ─────────────┐
     │Additional│  │ to Computer   │      │  Test Computer   │
     │  Staff  │   │    Media      │      │     Systems      │
     └────┬────┘   └───────────────┘      └────────┬─────────┘
          ▼                                        ▲
     ┌─ 13 ────┐  ┌─ 14  Plan and ┐        ┌─ 15 ──────┐
     │Train User│  │   Schedule    │───────▶│ Cut over to│
     │& Computer│  │   Operating   │        │ Computer  │
     │Ops Staff │  │  Procedures   │        │  System   │
     └─────────┘  └───────┬───────┘        └───────────┘
                          ▲
     ┌─ 16  Educate all ┐ │  ┌─ 17  Review ┐   ┌─ Decision ─┐
     │  Staff affected  │─┘  │   System    │──▶│to Computerise│
     │  by Computer's   │    │ Performance │   │   further ?  │
     │   Introduction   │    └─────────────┘   └──────────────┘
     └──────────────────┘
```

Figure 6.1   The Overall Implementation Plan

IMPLEMENTATION 95

involved; such meetings enable the project manager to re-schedule or re-assign activities on the spot, and allow those involved to consult one another regarding interdependent activities.

Design Computer Systems

Although the client may expect the supplier to provide computer systems, he cannot abdicate responsibility for their design and successful completion.

If the supplier is designing tailor-made systems it is particularly important that all the client's staff give their full cooperation. It can be very time-wasting if, for instance, the supplier's designer wishes to agree the form of the invoice with the chief accountant, and he is not available.

Even if packaged systems are being provided, it is important that the management who are going to be affected are available to agree that the package's requirements are feasible.

If necessary, a senior manager of the client should be available to give a ruling if there are any points on which the systems designer and the affected manager fail to agree.

Because systems development times can be very difficult to estimate this is an area that needs the strictest supervision. The implementation of packaged systems should be much easier to estimate and control than tailor-made systems.

Prepare Computer Site

Most modern minicomputers require very little in the way of preparation; but obviously, a site will have to be selected, and advice sought from the supplier regarding cabling, air filtration and so on.

Remember that terminals may require BT telephone lines to connect them.

Test Hardware

The hardware, once installed, will need to undergo standard acceptance tests before software is tested. This process is unlikely to take longer than a day or two unless unforeseen problems are encountered.

Agree Systems Specification

Once systems are designed, the written specifications need to be agreed by all the parties affected. This can be 'a point of no return' because it can be extremely difficult, time-consuming and costly to amend programs once they have been written and tested; therefore it is essential that the client goes through the specifications with the supplier extremely carefully at this time.

The System Specification should contain, as a minimum, the following information which should be rigorously checked for its correctness and completeness. It is advisable that at this stage the auditors grant their acceptance to the proposed system.

System Specification Contents

1 INTRODUCTION

   Brief Introduction to the System.

2 PROCEDURE SUMMARY

   2.1 Summary showing major changes and explaining principles of the new system.
   2.2 Overview of Inputs, Files, Processes and Outputs.
   2.3 System flowchart depicting in outline, the sequence of events in a system, showing the department or function responsible for each event.

3 PROCEDURE SPECIFICATIONS

   3.1 Computer Run Charts depicting the logical sequence and, where relevant, interrelationships of the computer routines to be performed, showing inputs, files and outputs.
   3.2 Computer Procedure Flowcharts depicting, in sequence, the operations and decisions in a computer procedure. This may take the form of a flowchart, a decision table or, in the case of a low-level procedure, a narrative description or arithmetical formula.
   3.3 Clerical procedures depicting, in sequence, the inputs, outputs and processes. Their interface with the computer procedures should also be shown.

4 DATA

    4.1 Inputs giving samples or mock-ups of input documents and screen layouts.

    4.2 Files (both computer and clerical) showing:
record layouts – field sizes, type of field, range, permitted values, etc.
file layouts – file contents, organisation and size.

    4.3 Outputs giving samples or mock-ups of output documents showing any pre-printed stationery to be used.

5 CONTROLS

    5.1 Audit trail.

    5.2 Security and Recovery procedures.

6 CHANGEOVER

    6.1 Timescales, critical activities and work loads.

    6.2 Acceptance schedules and estimated costs.

7 OPERATIONS

    7.1 Input/output volumes and frequencies with resultant operational requirements and equipment loadings.

    7.2 Work schedules.

Order Stationery, Computer Media, Peripherals

Having agreed the systems design, the various input and output documentation will require ordering from stationery suppliers. The systems suppliers will probably advise on this, as well as the requirements for disks, tapes, and so on which the computer system may require. There may also be a requirement for peripheral equipment such as bursters, decollators, guillotines and envelopers.

Delivery times for stationery, including checking and agreeing proofs, can be a time-consuming operation, for which adequate allowance must be made.

Re-Organise and Re-Deploy Staff where Necessary

The computer is unlikely to cause massive redundancies among your clerical staff, but it is a point that needs to be considered; and what management's strategy is going to be in regard to it.

Many jobs will certainly change, and due consideration needs to be given to the suitability of existing staff to new work. Many managements find that the introduction of the computer gives them an ideal opportunity to rationalise their organisations, to give them a more stream-lined work flow.

It follows, therefore, that the human element in any systems design is just as, if not more important than, the technical design.

Management should take care that any re-organisation as a result of the computer system has the full backing of their staff. One of the quickest routes to failure is to have staff who resent the changes brought about by the computer, and do not accept the requirements which the new system imposes.

Recruit Any Additional Staff

It is unlikely that any additional staff will be required, but this will depend on the suitability of the existing staff to carry out new work.

It should not be too difficult to retrain staff with anything like average ability as VDU and computer operators; but if the supplier recommends that some computer specialist staff are needed, recruitment will have to be considered.

Convert Files to Computer Media

All relevant records which the system requires the computer to hold (customer records, stock records, and so on) will have to be transferred to computer media, such as disks.

This can be a long process if many thousands of records are involved. Once the file layouts have been agreed with the system designer, a start can be made. A bureau could be used if the user is anxious to start before his own computer is installed.

As the records in their existing state probably do not conform with the required file layouts, they may have to be copied out onto special-purpose forms to assist the media operators. It is also highly probable that the existing records will not be able to be released from their existing files; in which case copying may need to be done on site. Temporary clerical staff may need to be brought in for this purpose.

IMPLEMENTATION

Volatile information, such as stock balances, will probably need to go on the computer immediately before going live. This is likely to be a concentrated exercise, perhaps over a weekend, if many records are involved.

Test Computer Systems

Once systems are designed and agreed, thorough tests will have to be carried out. This is usually done in stages. If packages are being supplied one can assume that the reliability of the package has already been tested and the user will merely want to test the acceptability of his own data. Where there are tailor-made systems, the testing will be more complex.

Once the reliability of the system has been tested, the user will need to provide historical data which has already gone through his manual system and for which the results are already known, so that he can satisfy himself that the computer can produce the same results. This stage should incorporate the testing of period-end and year-end procedures.

The next stage is a 'parallel run', during which the computer runs alongside the manual system, until the user is quite happy that the manual system can be entirely replaced. For a small organisation, this might involve overtime working with the computer carrying out the normal daily operation during an evening shift.

Train User and Computer Operations Staff

The supplier should provide training for everyone connected with the computer system, so that they are thoroughly acquainted with their new functions. This will mainly consist of training those actually operating the computer, those providing input data via VDUs, and those who are at the receiving end of the computer output, so that they know what to expect.

Plan and Schedule Operating Procedures

A daily routine will need to be organised for the computer and those affected by it. A regular schedule of work should be organised, with times when certain jobs are to be run. There will also be weekly jobs (payroll) and monthly jobs (customer statements, budgets, etc) which also need to be slotted into a regular timetable. Much of this will have to be considered when systems are designed and the new organisation is established.

Cut Over to Computer System

Once computer systems are thoroughly tested, a decision must be made to relinquish manual systems and go over entirely to the computer system.

Educate All Staff Affected by Computer's Introduction

In addition to training those directly involved with the computer, it is advisable that all those affected by the computer should have some knowledge of the system. It is worth carrying out this education programme to ensure that any mystique is dispelled from the computer, and that people are fully aware of its limitations. The simple point that the computer is entirely dependent on the people of the organisation to provide it with accurate information, in order that it can give accurate information, is one worth making.

Review System Performance

After the system has been installed, a formal review should be undertaken after a period of three to six months. This should have been agreed with the supplier beforehand, and could be viewed rather like the warranty period for a motor car. At the end of this period the client can discuss with the supplier whether the system is coming up to scratch; and if not, there may be an agreement that the supplier rectifies any problems which may have arisen.

If further systems are contemplated, it will probably be a point to decide whether the organisation is ready for further computerisation yet; or whether the present system needs a further settling-in period.

Part 2

Common Types of Computer Applications

7 Payroll

INTRODUCTION

All businesses require some type of payroll system. The employees expect to be paid on time and the Government requires that all employers maintain accurate records pertaining to Pay As You Earn (PAYE) tax and National Insurance (NI) payments. The PAYE and NI deductions are withheld from the employees' earnings and are paid to the Government. These and other deductions constitute the difference between the gross pay earned and the net pay received. For accounting purposes, most businesses maintain payroll records on all employees. These payroll records may be called the Payroll Ledger, which is subsidiary to the Nominal Ledger. The payroll totals such as gross pay, net pay, PAYE withholding, and NI withholding are included in the Nominal Ledger and are posted for each pay period.

Preparing a payroll requires collecting employee work hours, converting hours to gross earnings, and computing allowances, deductions and net pay. This is true of a computerised payroll just as much as for a manual payroll system. In fact a computerised payroll system operates in almost exactly the same way as its manual counterpart. Perhaps this is the reason why the payroll application is one of the oldest and most common business computer applications. However, there are many other reasons for computerising a payroll.

Of all the common accounting applications, payroll is perhaps the one with the highest number of repetitive calculations to be performed. It is also extremely important (certainly to the employee) that these calculations be done accurately. One thing a computer can do well is to carry out masses of repetitive calculations not only quickly, but also accurately.

Payroll was thus an obvious candidate for computerisation if for no other reason than that it virtually eliminated the intricate, error-prone and time-consuming calculations traditionally associated with the payroll function.

A payroll application however is not simply a matter of performing a lot of repetitive calculations. There are many other activities to be performed as by-products of the payroll calculation. These include accumulating summary data for Nominal Ledger reports; printing paypackets, cheques, payslips and other weekly, monthly and yearly reports; and making labour distribution and job costing measurements and reporting them. A computerised payroll system can not only print these reports (and many others beside) but also make them more complete, comprehensive and perhaps most importantly, more comprehensible. For, when all is said and done, it is just as important to the employees to understand how their pay is made up as to receive the actual pay itself. The final pay may only be a small part of the total payroll function, but to the employees it *is* the payroll. It means a lot to them. This is why a computerised payroll shows as much information as is possible on the payslip. It shows all the information employees need for auditing their own net and gross income; hours worked, pay rates, and deductions. The results are fewer misinterpretations and better informed employees.

In addition to producing all sorts of printed reports pertaining to the pay itself, a computerised payroll system often performs activities that might be viewed as personnel operations: sick leave and holiday entitlement and usage, home address maintenance, etc. While these activities enlarge the size of computer records used in the payroll system, they do not significantly increase the complexity of operating the overall application.

It is also common practice for year-to-date totals of gross, tax, net, etc, to be kept on the employee master file in addition to the current data. This means that end-of-year procedures such as those required for taxation purposes can be handled without the necessity for any further data entry.

For all these, and many other reasons, the payroll application has lent itself readily to computerisation. Had computerised payroll calculation and printing not become popular, then the computer may have been little understood and less in demand, no matter how good it was at processing data.

THE PAYROLL FILES

The master file used in payroll processing contains permanent as well as current data. Each record of this file holds such details as:

    Employee number

    Name

    Address

    Telephone number

    Pay location

    Start and termination dates

    Payment method (eg cash, cheque, bank deposit)

    Frequency (eg weekly, monthly)

    Standard hours

    Standard rate code

    Standard allowances and deductions

    Holiday and sick entitlement

    YTD gross, tax, net, etc.

The permanent portion of the file must be updated before current transactions (timesheets) are entered into the system, since information such as employee's rate of pay, accumulated holiday and National Insurance withholding is used to transform gross into net pay. Moreover, changes made to the master file are complex and require careful visual editing at data entry time, whereas current transactions entered from timesheets can be edited quite well by programmed tests. Therefore, prior to the actual processing of a payroll, the payroll office obtains data on new employees and on recent changes to existing employees. These changes are then entered through the video, and to maintain system integrity, all operator adjustments to the employee master file are logged to an audit file and printed for later scrutiny by management.

Figure 7.1 illustrates an audit trail report for a master file update. The report indicates any new employees and also every change made to an existing employee. When new employees are placed on the file, an appropriate word such as 'added' is prominently printed. When employee

RUN DATE: 13-JUL-80 04:50:14
NORTHWEST INDUSTRIES Pty Ltd
PAGE 001

EMPLOYEE MASTER FILE AUDIT TRAIL

EMP. NO.	SURNAME ADDRESS	INITS	GIVEN NAMES	LOC. STAFF IND. START	PAY DETAILS METHOD / FREQUENCY / STD HOURS / RATE CODE	ALLOW/DEDUCT	ACTION
1240	BLAIR 22 Harris Drive Charlestown TEL. 46 2314	GL	Garry Larry	1 S 15/ 5/76	M W 40.00 CLK1	8.56- 71 5.00 72 3.44- 40.00-	ADDED
1571	FREDRICKSON 33 Lebeilia Avenue, Ferngrove TEL. 065 67891	JD	Joan Debbie	1 S 6/ 6/76	M W 400.00 CLK0	6.50- 72 14.00 25.00-	ADDED
1571	FREDRICKSON 33 Lebeilia Avenue, Ferngrove TEL. 065 67891	JD	Joan Debbie	1 S 6/ 6/76	M W 40.00 CLK0	6.50- 72 14.00 25.00-	CHANGED
1571	FREDRICKSON 33 Lebeilia Avenue, Ferngrove TEL. 065 67891	JD	Joan Deborah	1 S 6/ 6/76	M W 40.00 CLK0	6.50- 72 14.00 25.00-	CHANGED
2263	SIMON 223 Pacific Drive, Belmont TEL. 45 6678	KR	Kenneth Raymond	2 S 12/ 4/78	M W 40.00 SMM1	3.88- 72 7.00 58 5.00 11.00- 8.50	ADDED
3189	THOMPSON 56 Gross Crescent Thornton TEL. 33 5645	JE	James Edward	2 S 13/12/77	M W 40.00 LAB0	7.00- 58 4.50- 72 5.00 8.50 55.00-	ADDED
4730	VAN HOOK 34 Industrial Drive Wickham TEL.	JW	Julio Wenceras	2 W 5/ 7/79	M W 40.00 LAB0	8.55 72 10.00-	ADDED
4770	Browne 67 Riverside Street, Hexham TEL. 67 5657	JD	John Douglas	2 W 15/ 4/77	M W 40.00 LAB0	8.80- 71 120.00- 5.00-	ADDED
4770	Browne 67 Riverside Street, Hexham TEL. 67 5657	JD	John Douglas	2 W 15/ 4/77	M W 40.00 LAB0	8.80- 71 120.00- 5.00-	CHANGED
4770	BROWNE 67 Riverside Street, Hexham TEL. 67 5657	JD	John Douglas	2 W 15/ 4/77	M W 40.00 LAB0	8.80- 71 120.00- 5.00-	CHANGED

Figure 7.1

records are deleted from the file, these are labelled 'deleted'. However, when an employee is terminated, the year-to-date and other master file information for the employee is usually left on the file at least until the end of the fiscal year, since periodic reports require the appearance of terminated employee records to reflect the entire year-to-date payroll balance. Therefore there is usually some provision for a termination date to indicate that an employee is no longer active. When employee records are adjusted in any way, these are labelled 'changed' on the audit report.

To allow full system flexibility, some payroll systems include a Pay Rates file to hold various types of base rates. Each pay rate is coded and a flexible description is provided to make payslips and reports more readable. For each rate (or award) the file maintains a standard base rate and a non-productive base rate for sick or compensation time. Standard sick leave hours are maintained against each award. One advantage of this approach is that if a pay rate should change, one entry will bring all affected employees up to date.

There may also be an Allowances and Deductions file containing an identifying code, a description, a before or after tax code, a flag to indicate whether it is an allowance or a deduction, and a frequency code. This allows for complete flexibility at data entry of timesheets, and allows the payslips and deduction registers to show full descriptions, making them much easier to understand.

INPUT TO THE PAYROLL SYSTEM

After changes to the payroll master file, the actual payroll run begins. Timesheets are submitted for data entry. This data entry procedure is the 'heart' of the system and allows for waged and salaried employees to be selected for payment. The pays can be produced weekly, fortnightly or monthly, as required, plus each employee can be paid by cash, cheque or bank deposit. To facilitate data entry the system can calculate the pay details automatically (salary), on an hourly basis (wages), in advance (for holidays, etc), manually (to allow complete override), or for terminating employees.

For salaried employees, who are paid a regular salary, no timesheet or other document is submitted for determination of hours worked. Rather, the employee master file contains standard salary information, and a standard rate code is used to compute gross pay – except when salary must be adjusted to compensate for an unusual situation, such as sick leave or vacation. In this case, a manual adjustment is required as input to processing.

For waged employees separate hours can be entered for each type of entry, and can include:

    Normal time

    Time and a half time overtime

    Double time

    Two and a half time overtime

    Triple time

    Public holiday

    Sick time and reason

    Annual leave

    Workers compensation

    Considerations, extras, allowances

    Manual adjustments

Ideally, information on employee hours is batch controlled. The normal control procedure is to total normal and overtime hours, and this total is then used to verify that the computer has actually received the correct timesheet figures.

A detailed transaction edit list can also be produced to validate all pay entries before proceeding to the calculation. Full editing facilities are then available to correct any problems.

All income tax amounts are calculated from a tax table which automatically accommodates for problems usually associated with annual leave, casual workers and partial pays. At data entry it is possible to select a number of allowances and/or deductions from the Allowances/Deductions file. These allowances and deductions can be applied before or after tax and the facility is available to have them apply weekly, fortnightly or monthly, on an automatic basis, or be entered as a 'one-off', if required.

PAYROLL 109

RUN DATE: 13-JUL-80 05:02:38 NORTH WEST INDUSTRIES Pty Ltd PAGE 001

PAY DETAILS EDIT TRANSACTION LISTING

PERIOD ENDING 11/07/80

LOC	EMPLOYEE NO.	NAME	TYPE	HOURS	CODE	DESC	RATE	AMOUNT		ALLOWANCE/DEDUCTION		GROSS	TAX	NET
1	1240	GL BLAIR	A	40.00 N	CLK1	Clerk 1st	5.6410	225.64	70	8.56-71	3.44			
				1.00 O	CLK1	Clerk 1st	5.6410	8.46	11	5.00 72	40.00-			
				1.00 2	CLK1	Clerk 1st	5.6410	11.28				250.38	51.58	146.80
1	1571	JD FREDRICKSON	A	40.00 N	CLK0	Typist	3.6604	146.42	70	6.50-72	25.00-			
				6.00 P	CLK1	Clerk 1st	5.6410	33.85	55	14.00		180.27	17.77	145.00
2	2263	KR SIMON	A	40.00 N	SMN1	Storeman	4.6600	186.40	71	3.88-72	11.00-			
									57	7.00 58	8.50			
									11	5.00		191.40	38.12	153.90
2	3189	JE THOMPSON	A	40.00 N	LAB0	Labourer	4.2315	169.26	57	7.00 58	8.50			
				5.00 2	LAB0	Labourer	4.2315	42.32	71	4.50-72	55.00-			
				3.00 D	LAB0	Labourer	4.2315	31.73	11	5.00		56.61	147.70	248.31
2	4730	JW VAN HOOK	A	40.00 N	LAB0	Labourer	4.2315	169.26	58	8.55 72	10.00-			
				3.00 O	LAB0	Labourer	4.2315	19.04				188.30	27.55	159.30
2	4770	JD BROWN	H	33.00 N	LAB0	Labourer	4.2315	139.64	70	8.80-71	5.00			
				7.00 S	LAB0	Labourer	4.0000	28.00	72	120.00-				
				25.00 O A	LAB1	Foreman	5.2300	196.13				363.77	94.27	135.70
	6 EMPLOYEES TOTAL HRS			233.00 N				1036.62						
				29.00 O				223.63						
	6 PAYS			2.00 2				53.60						
				3.00 D				31.73						
				6.00 P				33.85						
				7.00 S				28.00						
				284.00				1407.43				TOTAL NET		888.40

Figure 7.2

REPORTS FROM THE PAYROLL SYSTEM

One advantage of a computerised payroll is the facility to produce as many reports as required once the pays have been calculated. Some of these reports are:

Employee Master Listing

Payslips/Paypackets

Coinage Analysis

Deduction Register

Cheque Register

Bank Deposits Register

Pay Transactions Edit List

Year-to-Date Earnings Summary

Payroll Journal

They are described in more detail below:

The *Pay Details Edit Transaction Listing* (Figure 7.2) shows all time entries made for each pay, and is a very useful worksheet for checking data entry. It extends the payroll calculation in detail and highlights any mistakes or problems. These errors can be easily remedied before producing the actual pays.

All pay details are clearly presented on *paypackets, or payslips* for the benefit of the employees. Figure 7.3 shows a combined paypacket-payslip, with the pay details (time, base rate description, plus allowances and deductions) printed on the paypacket itself. Once the cash has been inserted into the envelope, the paypacket flap folds over the printed pay details so that confidentiality is maintained. One advantage of this approach is that standard 4" paypackets can be used. However, if some employees are to be paid directly into a bank account, then a separate pre-printed payslip may be preferred. These can often show more detail than a combined paypacket/payslip and may even be preferred for employees paid by cash.

As a permanent record of the current pay, a *Payroll Journal* (Figure 7.4) is produced detailing the payment amounts and summary hours for

PAYROLL

TYPE	HOURS	DESC.		RATE	AMOUNT
NORMAL	40.00	Clerk	1st	5.6410	225.64
OT 1.5	1.00	Clerk	1st	5.6410	8.46
OT 2	1.00	Clerk	1st	5.6410	11.28
		Bonus			5.00
		GROSS			250.38
		TAX			51.58
		Northwest Super Fun			8.56-
		A.B.C. Insurance			3.44-
		Bank			40.00-
		X.Y.Z.			
				NET	146.80

LOC. 1   EMP.NO. 1240
GL BLAIR

PERIOD ENDING 11/07/80 BY CASH

PRE-PRINTED PAYPACKETS or PAYSLIPS

TYPE	HOURS	DESC.		RATE	AMOUNT
NORMAL	40.00	Typist		3.6604	146.42
P.HOL.	6.00	Clerk	1st	5.6410	33.85
		GROSS			180.27
		TAX			17.77
		Vehicle Allowance			14.00
		Northwest Super Fun			6.50-
		Bank			25.00-
		X.Y.Z.			
				NET	145.00

LOC. 1   EMP.NO. 1571
JD FREDRICKSON

PERIOD ENDING 11/07/80 BY CASH

PRE-PRINTED PAYPACKETS or PAYSLIPS

Figure 7.3

RUN DATE: 13-JUL-80 05:04:25　　　　　　　　　　　　NORTHWEST INDUSTRIES Pty Ltd　　　　　　　　　　　　　　　　　　　　　　　　PAGE 001

PAYROLL JOURNAL

PERIOD ENDING 11/07/80

LOC	EMPLOYEE NO.	NAME		NORMAL	OVERTIME	SICK	HOLIDAY	OTHER	ALLOWANCES/DEDUCTIONS		GROSS	TAX	NET
1	1240	GL BLAIR	M	40.00 225.64	2.00 19.74				8.56 5.00	71 72	3.44-40.00-		
											250.38	51.58	146.80
1	1571	JD FREDRICKSON	M	40.00 146.42				6.00 33.85	6.50- 14.00	70 5	72	25.00		
											180.27	17.77	145.00

RUN DATE: 13-JUL-80 05:06:16　　　PAGE 010

PAYROLL JOURNAL

PERIOD ENDING 11/07/80

LOC	EMPLOYEE NO.	NAME		NORMAL	OVERTIME	SICK	HOLIDAY	OTHER	ALLOWANCES/DEDUCTIONS		GROSS	TAX	NET
2	4730	JW VAN HOOK	M	40.00 169.26	3.00 19.04				8.55	58 72	10.00-			
											188.30	27.55	159.30
2	4770	JD BROWN	M	33.00 139.64	25.00 196.13	7.00 28.00	70	8.80	8.30- 120.00-	90 72 91	5.00-			
											363.77	94.27	135.70

Figure 7.4

PAYROLL

NORTHWEST INDUSTRIES Pty Ltd   PAGE 001

RUN DATE: 13-JUL-80 06:04:31

A.B.C. INSURANCE LIST

PERIOD ENDING 11/07/80

LOC	NO.	EMPLOYEE NAME		AMOUNT
1	1240	GL	BLAIR	3.44
2	2263	KR	SIMON	3.88
2	3189	JE	THOMPSON	4.50
2	4770	JD	BROWNE	5.00
			TOTAL:	16.82

NORTHWEST INDUSTRIES Pty Ltd   PAGE 001

RUN DATE: 13-JUL-80 06:04:40

X.Y.Z. BANK LIST

PERIOD ENDING 11/07/80

LOC	NO.	EMPLOYEE NAME		AMOUNT
1	1240	GL	BLAIR	40.00
1	1571	JD	FREDRICKSON	25.00
2	2263	KR	SIMON	11.00
2	3189	JE	THOMPSON	55.00
2	4730	JW	VAN HOOK	10.00
2	4770	JD	BROWNE	120.00
			TOTAL:	261.00

Figure 7.5

each employee. The payroll journals can be filed as an historic reference of all pays for the current year. Summary totals are presented for each job or location, and company as well as a grand total to aid in auditing the pay.

Deposit/Cheque Registers itemise all employees who were not paid by cash, and facilitate bank deposits and cheque production.

A report is produced for every *Allowance* or *Deduction* category (Figure 7.5) that is used. Each report details employee location, number, name and amount, to help in preparation of returns to insurance companies, unions and other bodies.

8 Sales Ledger

INTRODUCTION

The Sales Ledger is subsidiary to the Nominal Ledger. Its purpose is to keep a record of each customer who owes money to the business and the amount he owes. The Nominal Ledger maintains a Sales Ledger account which reflects only the total of the Sales Ledger. The Sales Ledger on the other hand has all invoices and payments posted to it and the total of the new invoices and payments is posted to the Sales Ledger account in the Nominal Ledger (usually monthly) so that it remains in balance with the subsidiary ledger.

Some of the advantages of keeping the details in a subsidiary ledger are:

— not overburdening the Nominal Ledger with detail;

— maintaining greater control over the accounts receivable and their collection.

All sales for which customers owe payment are listed in the Sales Ledger. The details of each sale are found on the sales invoice and generally include:

Customer number

Invoice number

Invoice date

Amount of the invoice

Salesman responsible

Miscellaneous amount

Tax amount

Freight amount

All invoices for a customer are grouped together. As payments are made, they are applied to the customer's outstanding invoices. Generally each payment (ie cash receipt) is identified by:

Customer number

Receipt date

Cheque number

Amount received

Discount allowed

Invoices and payments represent the two main inputs into a Sales Ledger. However, should an invoice or payment be inadvertently posted to the wrong customer account, or some other error is detected, then a credit or debit memo is issued and the customer account amended accordingly. Thus we have identified four inputs into a Sales Ledger:

Invoice (Sale)

Payment (Cash receipt)

Credit memo

Debit memo

These inputs are processed in order to prepare a number of outputs including an up-to-date *Customer Statement* (usually monthly) and supporting reports. The most common report is called the *Aged Trial Balance*, which identifies customers who have fallen behind in their payments.

TYPES OF ACCOUNTS

There are two types of Sales Ledger systems:

— Open Item;

— Balance Forward.

An *open-item* Sales Ledger system keeps details of every sales invoice

SALES LEDGER

until such time as the invoice is paid in full. Customer statements show details not only for current monthly purchases, but also for any invoice that has not been paid in full. If payments or credits partially reduce the balance of an outstanding invoice, the net amount to be paid will be printed.

Customers can, and usually do, select the invoices to be paid when a cash payment is submitted. If a customer desires to protest a particular invoice, then this may be stipulated at the time of payment. The invoice in question then remains in the Sales Ledger file. Sometimes, a customer orders material and later returns it for credit. If the monthly statement is printed before a credit memo is processed, the invoice charge appears. The customer disregards this charge, knowing it will be accounted for by the next statement.

To encourage customers to indicate the invoices being paid when a cash payment is submitted, the monthly statement often has a detachable 'Remittance Stub' on the right hand side which gives a summary of each outstanding invoice (usually invoice number and amount). This can then be used as a Remittance Advice to accompany the cash payment, and if it is, then it is usual for the customer to indicate on the Remittance Stub those invoices being paid. If the remittance does not indicate the invoices being paid then the payment is usually posted against the oldest outstanding invoices.

In a *balance-forward* system the details for each month are not retained for reprinting on the customer statement the following month. Only the balance due is retained: hence the name balance forward or balance carry forward. Invoices are kept for only one month after the statement has been printed. If any are still unpaid after this period, they are totalled into a monthly balance, and further statements show only those outstanding monthly balances. Rather than just a single overdue amount, the unpaid balance is segregated by age: 30 days overdue, 60 days overdue, and greater than 90 days overdue. This ageing procedure may not have any great effect on the customer – if the customer is simply not paying bills, a large overdue balance is not threatening. However, the age and size of the overdue balance is important for collection activity. Accounts that are excessively overdue are given greater attention. Follow-up telephone calls or legal action may be initiated to collect the unpaid balance. Alternatively, the customer with excessive overdue balances may be put on a cash-only basis until all debts are paid.

To help maintain control over the credit a business extends to its customers, a periodic Aged Trial Balance report should be prepared from the Sales Ledger. This report lists the total amount in the Sales Ledger and the amount owed by each customer. It also categorises the invoices by the length of time they have been due. This categorising by length of time due is known as 'ageing'. The common ageing categories are:

1-30 days

31-60 days

61-90 days

Over 90 days

The Aged Trial Balance report helps the business to identify the payment habits of its customers.

COMPUTERISING THE SALES LEDGER

The computerised Sales Ledger system described in this chapter will use the open-item method. Before a Sales Ledger system can be implemented on a computer, each customer must be assigned a number by which the computer may reference them, allowing invoices to be stored on the computer and reported by customer number. A Customer Master file is also maintained containing customer number, customer name, 4 lines of invoice address and 4 lines of delivery address, customer type code (eg R = retailer, W = wholesaler, etc), salesman code, sales and cost-of-sales month-to-date (MTD) and year-to-date (YTD), taxable status, credit limit, and discount rate.

Transactions to the Sales Ledger system will record either new sales invoices or payments received from customers. Credit and debit adjustments are also catered for, and it is convenient to combine them with the sales invoices onto one transaction file, while the cash receipts are recorded onto another. There are many reasons for this approach. One is that a 'Sales Journal' (Figure 8.1) which shows details of all new sales invoices including credit and debit memos can be easily printed. Another is that in an open-item system the facility is available for a cash receipt to be posted against particular invoices and to this end, the computer system can either ask the operator to enter the invoice number(s) to which the payment applies or else display all the outstanding (or 'open') invoices on the video automatically and allow the operator to select which invoices to

SALES LEDGER

RUN DATE: 01-JAN-77　　　　　　　　　　　　　NORTH WEST INDUSTRIES Pty Ltd　　　　　　　　　　　　　PAGE 001

SALES JOURNAL

DOCUMENT TYPES:　1 = SALE (INVOICE)　3 = CR MEMO　4 = FINANCE CHARGE　5 = DEBIT MEMO

DOCUMENT NO	TYPE	DATE	CUSTOMER NO	NAME	SL MN	SALE AMOUNT	MISC AMOUNT	VAT AMOUNT	FREIGHT AMOUNT	TOTAL AMOUNT	COST AMOUNT	APL-TO DOC-NO
123456	1	31/12/76	10000	BETTER SERVICE CORP.	10	1,000.00	25.50	.00	50.00	1,0750.50	633.00	
123457	1	31/12/76	40000	NEIGHBORHOOD WOMEN'S CLUB	20	65.00	.00	3.90	.00	68.90*	40.00	
123458	1	31/12/76	20000	ACME DISTRIBUTORS, INC.	20	6,981.23	187.00	.00	476.50	7,644.73	4,198.32	
123459	3	31/12/76	30000	XYZ MANUFACTURING CO.	30	.00	.00	.00	50.00-	50.00-	.00	
123460	1	31/12/76	99999	CASH SALES FOP 31/12/76	0	167.40	.00	9.14	.00	176.54	92.50	
123461	5	31/12/76	10000	BETTER SERVICE CORP.	10	.00	45.00	.00	.00	45.00	.00	97623
				SALES SUB TOTALS:		8,213.63	212.50	13.04	526.50	8,965.67	4,963.82	
				CR MEMO SUB TOTALS:		.00	.00	.00	50.00-	50.00-	.00	
				FIN. CHARGE SUB TOTALS:		.00	.00	.00	.00	.00	.00	0
				DEBIT MEMO SUB TOTALS:		.00	45.00	.00	.00	45.00	.00	
				TOTALS:		8,213.63	257.50	13.04	476.50	8,960.67	4,963.82	

740751 = HASH OF　　20999 = HASH OF
　　DOCUMENT #S　　　　CUSTOMER #S

6 ENTRIES

Figure 8.1

RUN DATE: 01-JAN-77　　　　　　　　　NORTHWEST INDUSTRIES Pty Ltd　　　　　　　　　　　　　　　　　　　　　PAGE 001

CASH RECEIPTS JOURNAL

NAME	─────CUSTOMER─────	RECEIPT DATE	CHEQUE NO	A/R-AMOUNT RECEIVED	DISCOUNT ALLOWED	TOTAL-CR TO-CUS-ACC	APPLY-TO DOC-NO
10000	BETTER SERVICE CORP.	31/12/76	2746	493.92	10.08	504.00	96776
20000	ACME DISTRIBUTORS, INC.	31/12/76	1578	1,969.04	40.18	2,009.22	98551
30000	XYZ MANUFACTURING CO.	31/12/76	8723	476.89	.00	476.89	82096
		31/12/76	8723	1,479.40	.00	1,479.40	97623
		CHECK TOTALS:		1,956.29	.00	1,956.29	
30000	XYZ MANUFACTURING CO.	31/12/76	8724	4,398.95	89.77	4,488.72	109982
40000	NEIGHBORHOOD WOMEN'S CLUB	31/12/76	378	138.72	.00	138.72	
99999	CASH SALES FOR 31/12/76	31/12/76	0	167.40	.00	167.40	
	TOTALS			9,124.32	140.03	9,264.35	
22999 = HASH OF CUST NOS	TOTAL CASH RECEIVED:			9,124.32			
7 ENTRIES							

Figure 8.2

SALES LEDGER

pay. Yet another reason is that separating the cash receipts from the sales invoices facilitates the printing of a 'Cash Receipts Journal' (Figure 8.2) which shows the cash receipts and the invoice numbers to which they apply as well as any 'non-sales ledger' cash received. An example of the latter would be interest on cash invested, and in this and similar cases, the computer system would allow the operator to enter a Nominal Ledger account number at the time of entry, so that at the end of the month, when the Sales Ledger is interfaced with the Nominal Ledger, these amounts can be posted to their appropriate accounts. For all other intents and purposes, these 'non-sales ledger' amounts play no part in the Sales Ledger procedures.

In addition to the two transaction files mentioned previously, a third and perhaps more important transaction file is the Open-Item file. The sales transaction file and the cash receipts transaction file can be considered to be subsidiary to the Open-Item transaction file. Both files are posted to the Open-Item file periodically (at least once per month, depending on volumes), and as a by-product of this process, a Monthly Sales Summary file and a Monthly Cash Summary file are appended to. The MTD and YTD totals on the Customer Master File are also updated and after the Open-Item file has been appended to, the subsidiary transaction files are cleared ready for a new batch of transactions.

The Open-Item file is purged monthly, usually after the customer statements have been printed. When entering a credit/debit memo or cash receipt, the operator will have been asked for a specific invoice number to which the memo or cash receipt is to be applied in addition to supplying a separate document number. On purging the Open-Item file, all credit/debit memos and cash receipts are matched with the invoices to which they apply, and the invoices either deleted, or else adjusted to show any increase or decrease in the amount. At the end of this purging process, all that should remain on the Open-Item file are those outstanding invoices which have not been paid in full.

At any stage during the month, an 'Aged Trial Balance' report (Figure 8.3) can be produced, either for all customers or for selected customers. At the option of the operator, the detail within each customer may be suppressed, thereby showing only the summary aged subtotals for each customer. In both cases, the report categorises the 'ages' of the invoices such that those that appear in the 1-30 day category are dated during the current month, and those in the 31-60 day category are dated

RUN DATE: 01-JAN-77
NORTHWEST INDUSTRIES Pty Ltd
PAGE 001

ACCOUNTS RECEIVABLE AGED TRIAL BALANCE

AS OF 01/01/77

DOCUMENT TYPES: 1 = SALE (INVOICE) 2 = PAYMENT 3 = CR MEMO 4 = FINANCE CHARGE 5 = DEBIT MEMO

CUSTOMER		DOCUMENT		APPLY	SALE-AMT/	OTHER-CHGS/		AGED DOCUMENT TOTAL		
NO NAME	TYPE	DATE	NO	TO-DOC	CASH-RECD	DISC-ALLOWD	CURRENT	31-60 DAYS	61-90 DAYS	OVER-90 DAYS
10000 BETTER SERVICE CORP.	1	22/10/76	93788		267.71	278.90			546.61	
	1	22/11/76	95890		1,888.72	300.00		2,188.72		
	1	22/12/76	96776		504.00	.00	504.00			
	2	12/12/76	5014	93788	546.61	.00				
	2	12/12/76	5014	95890	2,147.67	41.05				
	1	12/12/76	123456		1,000.00	75.50	1,075.50			
	5	31/12/76	123461	0	.00	45.00	45.00			
CUSTOMER TOTAL =	1,624.50				CUSTOMER AGED SUB TOTALS:		1,624.50	.00	546.61	.00
CREDIT LIMIT =	3,000.00									
2000 ACME DISTRIBUTORS, INC.	1	12/02/76	98551		2,009.23	389.23	2,398.46			
	1	12/31/76	123458		6,981.23	663.50	7,644.73			
CUSTOMER TOTAL =	10,043.19				CUSTOMER AGED SUB TOTALS:		10,043.19	.00	.00	.00
CREDIT LIMIT =	10,000.00			*** LIMIT EXCEEDED ***						
30000 XYZ MANUFACTURING CO.	5	13/09/76	82096		476.89	.00				476.89
	1	30/10/76	97623		1,479.40	50.00			1,529.40	
	1	14/12/76	109982		3,988.72	500.00	4,488.72			
	1	21/12/76	117623		4,099.23	379.00	4,478.23			
	3	31/12/76	123459	97623	50.00-	50.00-			50.00-	
	4	12/31/76	123176		.00	29.34	29.34			
CUSTOMER TOTAL =	10,952.58				CUSTOMER AGED SUB TOTALS:		8,996.29	.00	1,479.40	476.89
CREDIT LIMIT =	20,000.00									
40000 NEIGBORHOOD WOMEN'S CLUB	1	27/11/76	940092		130.80	7.92	138.72-	138.72		
	2	31/12/76	378		138.72	.00	68.90			
	1	31/12/76	123457		65.00	3.90				
CUSTOMER TOTAL =	68.90				CUSTOMER AGED SUB TOTALS:		68.90	138.72	.00	.00
CREDIT LIMIT =	200.00									
50000 UNIVERSAL ADVERTISING CO.	1	27/10/76	96523		651.20	40.00		513.64	691.20	
	1	25/11/76	100054		490.08	23.56				
	2	12/12/76	1672	96523	691.20-	.00			691.20-	
	4	11/12/76	123176		.00	7.70	7.70			
CUSTOMER TOTAL =	521.34				CUSTOMER AGED SUB TOTALS:		7.70	513.64	.00	.00
CREDIT LIMIT =	500.00			*** LIMIT EXCEEDED ***						
GRAND TOTAL =	23,210.51				GRAND AGED SUP TOTALS:		20,740.58	513.64	1,479.40	476.89

Figure 8.3

SALES LEDGER

RUN DATE: 01-JAN-77　　　　　　　　　　　　　NORTHWEST INDUSTRIES Pty Ltd　　　　　　　　　　　　　PAGE 001

ACCOUNTS RECEIVABLE AGED TRIAL BALANCE SUMMARY

AS OF 01/01/77

	CUSTOMER		TOTAL	CREDIT		AGED-SUB-TOTALS			OVER
NO	NAME		AMT-DUE	LIMIT	CURRENT	31-60-DAYS	61-90-DAYS	OVER-90-DAYS	CRLM
10000	BETTER SERVICE CORP.		1,624.50	3,000.00	1,624.50	.00	.00	.00	
20000	ACME DISTRIBUTORS, INC.		10,043.19	10,000.00	10,043.19	.00	.00	.00	*
30000	XYZ MANUFACTURING CO.		10,952.58	20,000.00	8,996.29	.00	1,479.40	476.89	
40000	NEIGHBORHOOD WOMEN'S CLUB		68.90	200.00	68.90	.00	.00	.00	
50000	UNIVERSAL ADVERTISING CO.		521.30	500.00	7.70	513.64	.00	.00	*
	GRAND TOTALS:		23,210.51		20,740.58	513.64	1,479.40	476.89	

Figure 8.3 (cont)

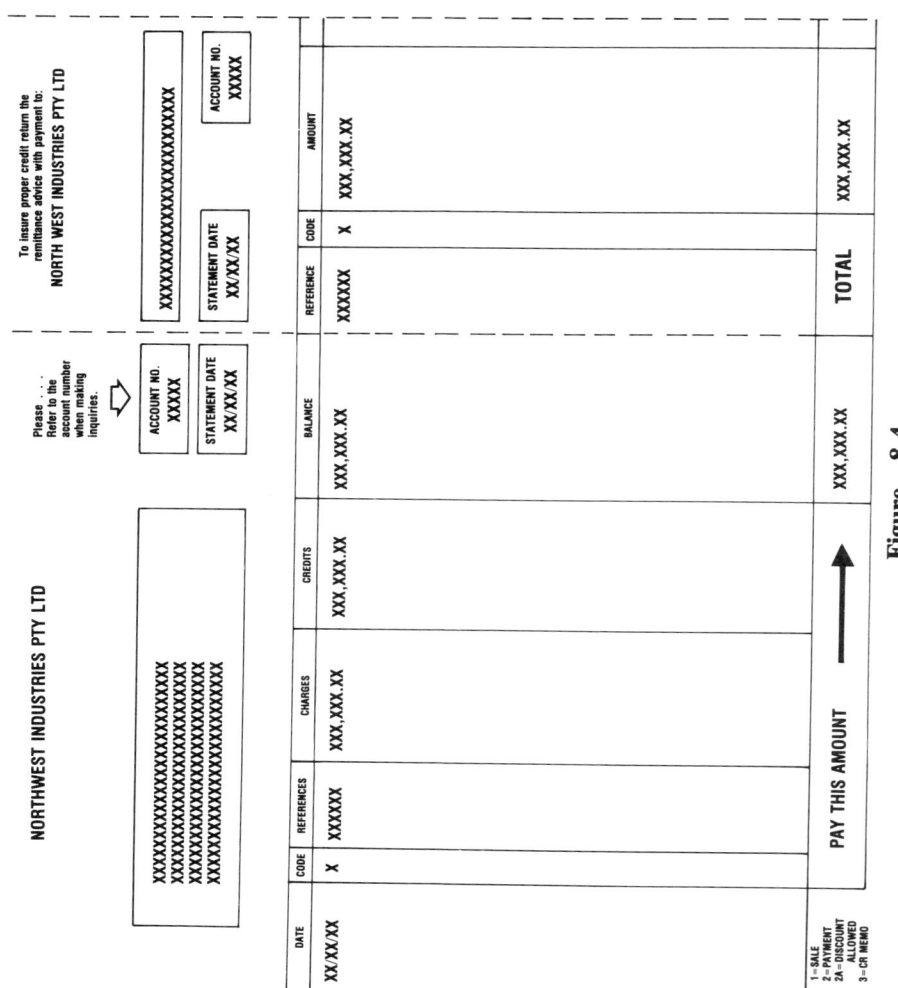

Figure 8.4

SALES LEDGER

RUN DATE: 01-JAN-77 NORTHWEST INDUSTRIES PTY LTD PAGE 001

MONTHLY SALES SUMMARY

TRX TYPES: 1 = SALE (INVOICE)   3 = CR MEMO   4 = FINANCE CHARGE   5 = DEBIT MEMO

POSTING DATE	TRX TYPE	SALE AMOUNT	MISC CHARGES	SALES TAX	FREIGHT AMOUNT	TOTAL SALES
03/12/76	1	7,872.32	88.23	138.82	123.00	8,222.37
03/12/76	3	600.00-	.00	30.00-	.00	630.00-
10/12/76	1	29,988.54	578.23	409.09	870.50	31,846.36
10/12/76	1	8,102.12	40.00	41.09	312.50	8,495.71
10/12/76	3	3,078.23-	77.12-	209.90-	150.60-	3,515.85-
10/12/76	5	.00	50.00	.00	.00	50.00
17/12/76	1	8,102.12	40.00	41.09	312.50	8,495.71
24/12/76	1	11,456.52	578.23	409.09	870.50	13,314.34
24/12/76	3	340.00-	.00	30.00-	.00	370.00-
31/12/76	1	8,213.63	212.50	13.04	526.50	8,965.67
31/12/76	3	.00	.00	.00	50.00-	50.00-
31/12/76	4	.00	37.04	.00	.00	37.04

SALES:		73,735.25	1,537.19	1,052.22	3,015.50	79,340.16
CR MEMOS:		4,018.23-	77.12-	269.90-	200.60-	4,565.85-
FIN CHGS:		.00	37.04	.00	.00	37.04
DR MEMOS:		.00	50.00	.00	50.00-	50.00

| TOTALS: | | 69,717.02 | 1,547.11 | 782.32 | 2,814.90 | 74,861.35 |

RUN DATE: 01-JAN-77 NORTHWEST INDUSTRIES PTY LTD PAGE 001

MONTHLY CASH RECEIPTS SUMMARY

POSTING DATE	A/R-AMOUNT RECEIVED	DISCOUNT ALLOWED	TOTAL-CREDIT TO-A/R	MISC-AMOUNT RECEIVED	G/L ACCT-NO
03/12/76	5,899.23	27.88	5,927.11	.00	
03/12/76				69.00	3300-100
10/12/76	13,009.82	156.72	13,166.54	.00	
17/12/76	6,712.90	40.09	6,752.99	.00	
17/12/76				167.50	3200-100
24/12/76	15,990.23	209.87	16,200.10	.00	
31/12/76	9,124.32	140.03	9,264.35	.00	

| TOTALS: | 50,736.50 | 574.59 | 51,311.09 | 236.50 | |

TOTAL CASH RECEIVED = 50,973.00

Figure 8.5

for the preceding month.

Prior to the printing of the monthly customer statements, finance charges (if applicable) are calculated as a set percentage on outstanding invoices or else manually calculated and entered through the video. These charges are then added as extra transactions to the Open-Item file and also the Monthly Sales Summary file. They will therefore appear on the Customer Statement as separate entries to be recalculated the following month if the outstanding invoices are not paid in full.

The printing of Customer Statements (Figure 8.4) is usually done at the end of the month, but as the statement date is entered through the video, there is no reason why they could not be printed at any time. They can be printed for all or for selected customers, and aged subtotals (ie totals of outstanding invoices aged by month) may optionally be shown at the bottom of the statements. The right hand side of the statement is a Remittance Advice stub. It is perforated for tear off and is designed to be used by the customer to indicate the invoices being paid and to be returned by the customer with his payment.

The contents of the Monthly Sales Summary file are printed at the end of the month in the form of a 'Monthly Sales Summary' report (Figure 8.5), showing totals of Sales invoices, Credit and Debit Memos, and Finances Charges for each posting date within the month. A 'Monthly Cash Receipts Summary' report is produced from the monthly Cash Receipts Summary file in a similar fashion. The details on both the Monthly Sales Summary file and the Monthly Cash Receipts Summary file are then added to the Sales Ledger Interface file for later posting to the Nominal Ledger. The two summary files are then cleared.

Various Sales Analysis reports such as 'Sales Analysis by Customer' and 'Sales Analysis by Salesman' can be produced at any time simply by running the appropriate program using the Customer Master File.

9 Purchase Ledger

INTRODUCTION

The purpose of a Purchase Ledger system is to pay for purchases or services received from suppliers. Most services and supplies are purchased 'on credit', rather than by cash payment at the time of purchase. Thus a number of unpaid invoices accrue to a supplier. A Purchase Ledger system is the logical opposite of a Sales Ledger system – the company in this case is the customer rather than the supplier or vendor. However, like a Sales Ledger system, it is also subsidiary to the Nominal Ledger, and summary information is posted from the Purchase Ledger to expense accounts in the Nominal Ledger at frequent intervals.

All purchases by the company for which payment is owed are listed in the Purchase Ledger. The details of each purchase are found on the supplier's invoice and therefore all invoices for a supplier are grouped together. Payment of these outstanding invoices is normally made when they become due. It is important in a Purchase Ledger system to determine when to pay as well as what amount to pay. When to pay is based on a number of factors, but the main two are the *invoice due date* and the *stated discount policy*.

The *invoice due date* is the date the invoice is expected to be paid by and is either printed on the supplier invoice or else is determined by the stated terms of payment. For example, the terms of payment may state 30 days net, which means payment is expected within 30 days of the invoice date. Obviously, the supplier would prefer to have his invoices paid as soon as possible, since he in turn needs the money to satisfy his own creditors. To encourage prompt payment, most suppliers allow their customers *cash discounts* for paying an invoice within a specified time. This discount is usually about 2 per cent of the total bill, although it can be much more. Freight charges are frequently excluded in the calculation of a cash discount, since suppliers must pay the full freight amount. Some suppliers also attempt to collect interest for late payment as another method of forcing prompt payment, although in practice this is usually not very successful.

Thus in determining when to pay, it might appear wise to pay every invoice promptly in order to obtain the cash discount, thereby reducing the cost of the purchased goods. Most of the time this is what happens. Not every invoice, however, should be paid as soon as possible, nor should every discount be taken. Cash flow considerations mean that management is concerned to allocate available cash to whatever gives the maximum return on investment. The longer the payment of an invoice is delayed, the longer that amount of money is available for other purposes. This delay is often viewed as an interest-free, short-term loan from the supplier. However, delaying payments obviously means losing the prompt payment discount, and as this discount can often be tantamount to an annual rate of interest of 36 per cent, such practice should be weighed up against the possibility of borrowing the cash to pay the invoices on time. Whatever procedure is used in practice, it is important that any Purchase Ledger system should be able to report on how much money is due to the suppliers, when it is due, and the discounts to be saved by prompt payment.

INPUT TO THE SYSTEM

Supplier invoices constitute the main input into a computerised Purchase Ledger system. There are, however, other types of inputs such as *credit notes* and *manual cheques* which may need to be processed from time to time. When goods are returned or an invoice is miscalculated, then a credit note will be sent from the supplier and will be entered into the Purchase Ledger system to reduce the total amount owed to that supplier. Manual cheques are entered into the system so that the Cheque Register report can show the details of cheques which have been written by hand as well as those printed by the computer. This facilitates reconciliation with bank statements and other accounting procedures. The number of credit notes and manual cheques is normally very low, whereas there are usually a large number of supplier invoices to process through a Purchase Ledger system. For this reason, it is often common practice to distribute invoice totals to a number of Nominal Ledger expense accounts at the data entry

PURCHASE LEDGER

RUN DATE: 01-JAN-77 NORTHWEST INDUSTRIES PTY. LTD. PAGE 001

PURCHASE LEDGER VOUCHER REGISTER

VOUCHER NO.	NO.	VENDOR NAME	NO.	INVOICE DATE	AMOUNT	NON-DISC AMOUNT	DISC	DUE DATE	CHEQUE NO.	DISTRIBUTION N/L-ACCT	DISTRIBUTION AMOUNT
345678	4000	READY QUICK PRINTERS	7723	22/12/76	55.79	3.11	2.0%	31/12/76		4100-000	55.79
										4900-000	3.11
345679	1000	SUPERIOR DISTRIBUTORS	SD 19823	25/12/76	331.75	18.82	2%.0	31/12/76		4400-000	312.93
										4900-000	18.82
345680	7000	TELECOM	8812312	10/12/76	587.82	.00	0.0%	31/12/76		4500-000	587.82
345681	8000	LANDMARK REALTY MANAGEMENT	LM 5723	15/12/76	1,750.00	.00	0.0%	10/01/77		4600-000	1,400.00
										4200-000	127.00
										4300-000	223.00
345682	2000	BETTER OFFICE SUPPLY CO	8823	23/12/76	52.90	.00	0.0%	23/12/76	2883	4400-000	49.95
										4900-000	2.95
		4 REGULAR ENTRIES	REGULAR TOTAL (NET CHANGE TO P/L):		2,728.47					REGULAR DISTRIBUTION TOTAL:	2,728.47
		1 PREPAID ENTRIES	PREPAID TOTAL (NET CHANGE TO CASH)		52.90					PREPAID DISTRIBUTING TOTAL:	52.90
		5 TOTAL ENTRIES	GRAND INVOICE TOTAL:		2,781.37					GRAND N/L DISTRIBUTION TOTAL:	2,781.37

Figure 9.1

stage in order to avoid duplication of effort. Entering the Nominal Ledger account numbers to which each supplier invoice is to be distributed means that Purchase Ledger data entry takes longer than it would otherwise, but saves data entry time overall, because the same details do not then have to be entered directly into the Nominal Ledger as journal entries. The summary expense account totals can be interfaced regularly with the Nominal Ledger in a manner similar to that used for the Payroll and Sales Ledger systems. This procedure not only saves time, but also means that fewer errors are likely to find their way through to the Nominal Ledger.

In addition to the Nominal Ledger account numbers affected, the data entered for each supplier invoice includes:

Voucher number

Supplier number

Invoice number (one invoice to a voucher)

Invoice date

Invoice amount

Discount percentage or amount (if applicable)

Due date

The 'voucher number' is automatically assigned to each invoice as it is entered. For manual cheques, the cheque number and cheque date are also entered. The invoice details are then printed in a 'Purchase Ledger Voucher Register' (Figure 9.1) which simply shows all the data entered at data entry, plus totals.

THE PURCHASE LEDGER SYSTEM

There are three main files in the computerised Purchase Ledger system described in this chapter:

— Supplier Master file;

— New Purchase Ledger Transactions file;

— Purchase Ledger Pending Invoice file.

The Supplier Master file contains (for each supplier): supplier number, name, 4 lines of address, total amount billed (YTD) and the number of vouchers (YTD). The New Transactions file contains the data which was

PURCHASE LEDGER

RUN DATE: 01-JAN-77   NORTHWEST INDUSTRIES PTY LTD   PAGE 001

PURCHASE LEDGER AGED TRIAL BALANCE
AS OF 31/12/76

| VENDOR | | VOUCHER | INVOICE | | | AGED INVOICE AMOUNT | | | DISCOUNT | DUE |
NO	NAME	NO	NO	DATE	CURRENT	31-60 DAYS	61-90 DAYS	OVER-90 DAYS	AMOUNT	DATE
1000	SUPERIOR DISTRIBUTORS	308121	SD 99232	01/11/76	665.03				12.44	31/11/76
		318723	SD 99962	12/11/76	197.03				3.94	21/11/76
		345679	SD 19823	25/12/76					6.26	31/12/76
	VENDOR: TOTAL 1,193.81		VENDOR SUBTOTALS:			331.75	.00		22.64	
4000	READY QUICK PRINTERS	298712	6554	10/10/76			15.90		.32	10/11/76
		345678	7723	22/12/76	58.90				1.12	31/12/76
	VENDOR TOTAL: 74.80		VENDOR SUBTOTALS:		58.90		15.90		1.44	
6000	SMITH & JONES	308823	110576	05/11/76	1,180.00				.00	31/11/76
		308823	PARTIAL	10/12/76	590.00-				.00	31/12/76
	GRAND TOTAL: 4,251.43		GRAND SUBTOTALS:		2,042.06		15.90	.00	24.08	

PURCHASE LEDGER AGED TRIAL BALANCE SUMMARY
AS OF 31/12/76

| VENDOR | | | AGED-SUB-TOTALS | | | VENDOR | VALID | NET |
NO	NAME	CURRENT	31-60 DAYS	61-90 DAYS	OVER 90 DAYS	TOTAL	DISCOUNTS	TOTAL
1000	SUPERIOR DISTRIBUTORS	331.75	862.06	.00	.00	1,193.81	6.26	1,187.55
4000	READY QUICK PRINTERS	58.90	.00	15.90	.00	74.80	1.12	73.68
6000	SMITH & JONES	.00	590.00	.00	.00	590.00	.00	590.00
7000	TELECOM	587.82	.00	.00	.00	587.82	.00	587.82
8000	LANDMARK REALTY MANAGEMENT	1,805.00	.00	.00	.00	1,805.00	.00	1,805.00
5 VENDORS GRAND TOTALS:		2,193.47	2,042.06	15.90	.00	4,251.43	7.38	4,244.05

Figure 9.2

entered at data entry, and the first step after printing the Purchase Ledger Voucher Register is to strip off the Nominal Ledger account information. This information is merged with the existing Interface file for later posting to the Nominal Ledger. The remaining data from the New Transactions file is used to update the YTD fields on the Supplier Master file and is then merged with the Pending Invoice file. Once this has been done, the New Transactions file is cleared, ready for a new batch of invoices, credit notes and manual cheques.

The Pending Invoice file can be used at any time for the printing of the 'Purchase Ledger Aged Trial Balance' (Figure 9.2), either for all or for selected vendors. Ageing is by invoice date. The detail within each vendor may be suppressed, thereby showing only the summary aged subtotals for each vendor. Another very useful report for management is the 'Cash Requirements Report' (Figure 9.3) which can be printed at any time, but is usually printed just before the end of the month, or whenever cheques are normally written. It allows for a specific due date to be entered, and then the report shows all those invoices (by vendor) due to be paid on or before the specified due date, as well as any discounts gained if payment is made on the specified payment date. If the total cash available is less than the total cash required, then it is possible to change the due dates on some of the invoices so that they do not qualify for payment within the current month.

The actual payment of pending invoices may be by either deferral or selection. In the deferral method, all invoices prior to the specified due date except those specifically deferred are paid. Deferral may be for an entire vendor, or for selected invoices within a vendor. In the selection method, only those invoices specifically selected are paid. Partial payments may be made in either method. As a final check before the actual cheques are printed, a 'Pre-Cheque Writing Report' can be printed showing the invoices by vendor that are to be paid. Adjustments can still be made at this late stage, prior to the cheque printing run.

The cheque printing run normally combines the remittance advice voucher with the pre-printed cheque. The remittance advice portion of the printed cheque would list all invoices being paid by the cheque and the net amount for each invoice after the discount. This information helps the vendor to reconcile the cheque with his own receivable records. Figure 9.4 shows a stub-over-cheque format (perforated to facilitate separation), although a cheque-over-stub format is also quite common.

PURCHASE LEDGER

RUN DATE: 01-JAN-77
NORTHWEST INDUSTRIES PTY LTD
PAGE 001

CASH REQUIREMENTS REPORT

AS OF 31/12/76 FOR PAYMENT ON 31/12/76

VENDOR NO	NAME	VOUCHER NO	INVOICE NO	INVOICE DATE	DAYS AGED	DUE DATE	INVOICE AMOUNT	DISCOUNT VALID	DISCOUNT LOST	NET AMOUNT	NOTES
1000	SUPERIOR DISTRIBUTORS	308121	SD 9923	01/11/76	60	31/11/76	665.03		12.44	665.03	
		318723	SD 9996	17/11/76	44	31/11/76	197.03		3.94	197.03	
		345679	SD 19823	25/12/76	6	31/12/76	331.75	6.26		325.49	
						VENDOR TOTALS:	1,193.81	6.26	16.38	1,187.55	
4000	READY QUICK PRINTERS	298712	6554	10/10/76	81	10/11/76	15.90		.32	15.90	
		345678	7723	22/12/76	9	31/12/76	58.90	1.12		57.78	
						VENDOR TOTALS:	74.80	1.12	.32	73.68	
6000	SMITH & JONES	308823	110576	05/11/76	56	31/11/76	1,180.00	.00	.00	1,180.00	
		308823	PARTIAL PAID ON 10/12/76				590.00-			590.00-	
						VENDOR TOTALS:	590.00	.00	.00	590.00	
7000	TELECOM	345680	8812312	10/12/76	21	31/12/76	587.82	.00	.00	587.82	
						VENDOR TOTALS:	587.82	.00	.00	587.82	
8000	LANDMARK REALTY MANAGEMENT	328823	LM 5182	03/12/76	28	31/12/76	55.00	.00	.00	55.00	
						VENDOR TOTALS:	55.00	.00	.00	55.00	

TOTAL ALL VENDORS: 2,501.43   7.38   16.70   TOTAL CASH REQUIRED: 2,494.05

Figure 9.3

Figure 9.4

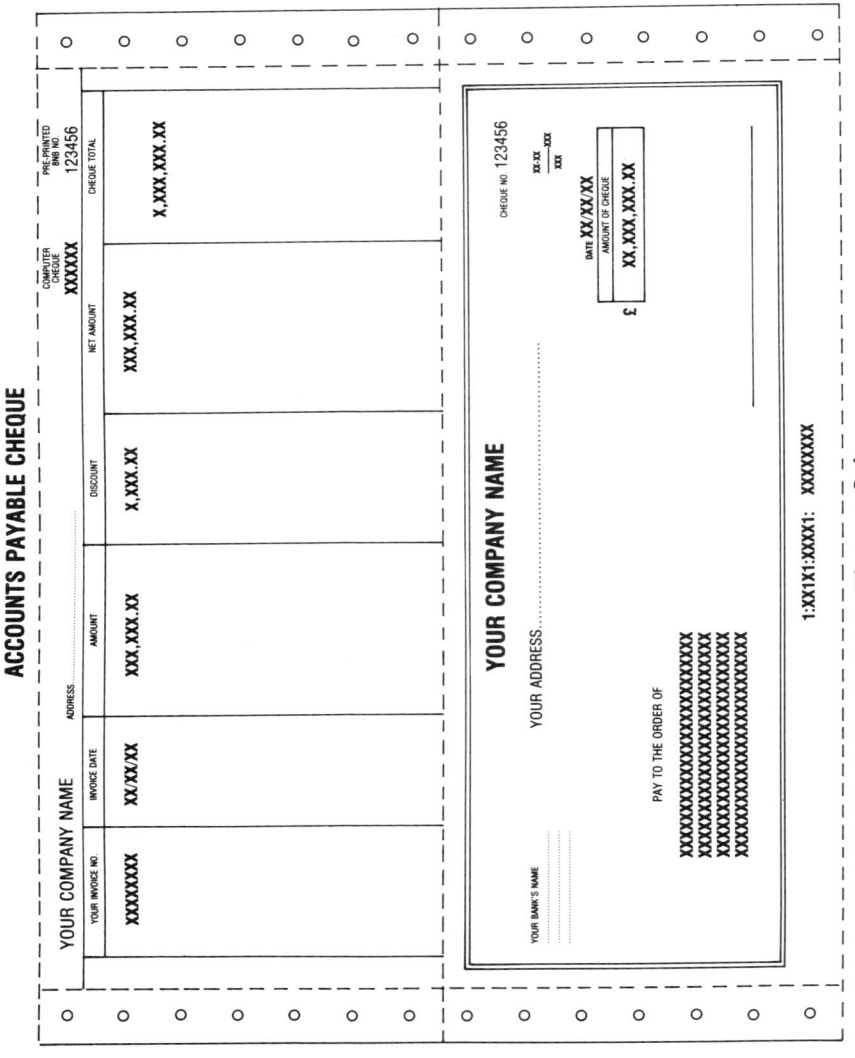

PURCHASE LEDGER

One important factor in the design of cheques in a computerised Purchase Ledger system is the printing of the cheque number. This number must be unique to each cheque. A common practice is to pre-print the cheque number; in other words to have the cheque supplier place the number on the cheque. The number is large and as the example in Figure 9.4 shows, can be printed using special characters which enable the number to be easily read by Optical Character Reader (OCR) machine. This is perhaps the main reason why the banks prefer pre-printed cheque numbers.

Unfortunately, pre-printed cheque numbers can cause more problems than they solve. The starting cheque number must be entered through a video, and if something malfunctions during cheque printing and it becomes necessary to reprint certain cheques, then another starting cheque number must be entered. This means that the cheque register when printed would then show a sequence of cheque numbers with a gap in the middle, or even worse still, a series of gaps. There are also one or two cheques wasted at the beginning of every cheque printing run and perhaps another cheque or two destroyed at the end of printing. Thus a consecutive run of cheque numbers will not be possible even if nothing malfunctions during the cheque printing run. This last problem however is not insurmountable, in that it is possible to sellotape a number of blank cheque forms onto the beginning of a run of cheques, and to use them for printing alignment rather than actual pre-printed cheques.

The alternative is to use the computer to print the cheque number together with the other information printed on the cheque. If something malfunctions during cheque printing, the print program can be restarted, and the cheque numbers of those cheques to be reprinted can be re-used. Thus every consecutive number can be used. Whichever approach is adopted, it should be remembered that the design of a remittance advice-cheque is an important part of the preparation for a computerised Purchase Ledger system, and should not be left until after the computer has been installed.

After the cheques have been printed, a 'Cheque Register' (Cash Disbursements Journal) is printed (Figure 9.5) showing details of all invoices paid (by vendor) on each cheque. Any manual cheques entered since the last Cheque Register was printed are also automatically shown in this report. It is at this stage that the Pending Invoice file is purged, and all invoices which have been paid in full are removed from the file.

RUN DATE: 01-JAN-77　　　　　　　　　　　　　　　NORTHWEST INDUSTRIES PTY LTD　　　　　　　　　　　　　　　PAGE 001

PURCHASE LEDGER CHEQUE REGISTER

CHEQUE NO	CHEQUE DATE	NO	NAME — VENDOR	VOUCHER NO	VENDOR INVOICE #	INVOICE DATE	INVOICE AMOUNT	DISCOUNT AMOUNT	CHEQUE AMOUNT
2883	23/12/76	2000	BETTER OFFICE SUPPLY CO	345687	8823	23/12/76	52.90	.00	52.90
1 MANUAL CHEQUES						TOTAL MANUAL CHEQUES:	52.90	.00	52.90
7762	31/12/76	1000	SUPERIOR DISTRIBUTORS	308121	SD 99232	01/11/76	665.03	.00	665.03
				318723	SD 99962	17/11/76	197.03	.00	197.03
				345679	SD 19823	25/12/76	331.75	6.26	325.49
						CHEQUE TOTALS:	1,193.81	6.26	1,187.55
7763	31/12/76	4000	READY QUICK PRINTERS	298712	6554	10/10/76	15.90	.00	15.90
				345678	7723	22/12/76	58.90	1.12	57.78
						CHEQUE TOTALS:	74.80	1.12	73.68
7764	31/12/76	6000	SMITH & JONES	308823	110576	05/11/76	1,180.00	.00	1,180.00
				308823	PART PAID ON	12/10/76	590.00-	.0	590.00-
						CHEQUE TOTALS:	590.00	.00	590.00
7765	31/12/76	7000	TELECOM	345680	8812317	10/12/76	587.82	.00	587.82
7766	31/12/76	8000	LANDMARK REALTY MANAGEMENT	328823	LM 5182	03/12/76	55.00	.00	55.00
5 COMPUTER CHEQUES						TOTAL COMPUTER CHEQUES:	2,501.43	7.38	2,494.05
6 MANUAL AND COMPUTER CHEQUES						TOTAL ALL CHEQUES:	2,554.33	7.38	2,546.95

Figure 9.5

PURCHASE LEDGER 137

RUN DATE: 01-JAN-77 NORTHWEST INDUSTRIES PTY LTD PAGE 001

PURCHASE LEDGER G1/L DISTRIBUTION CROSS REFERENCE

FOR THE PERIOD ENDING 31/12/76

EXPENSE-ACCOUNT NO	DESCRIPTION	VOUCHER NO	VENDOR NO	INVOICE NO	INVOICE DATE	AMOUNT
4100-000	ADVERTISING	298712	4000	6554	10/10/76	15.90
		345678	4000	7723	22/12/76	55.79
				EXPENSE ACCOUNT TOTAL:		71.69
4200-000	HEAT, POWER AND LIGHT	328823	8000	LM 5182	03/12/76	55.00
		345681	8000	LM 5723	15/12/76	127.00
				EXPENSE ACCOUNT TOTAL:		182.00
4300-000	INSURANCE	345681	8000	LM 5723	15/12/76	223.00
4400-000	OFFICE SUPPLIES	308121	1000	SD 9923	01/11/76	627.11
		318723	1000	SD 9996	17/11/76	186.05
		345679	1000	SD 19823	25/12/76	312.93
		345682	2000	8823	23/12/76	49.95
				EXPENSE ACCOUNT TOTAL:		1,176.04
4500-000	TELEPHONE	308823	6000	110576	05/11/76	80.00
		345680	7000	8812312	10/12/76	587.82
				EXPENSE ACCOUNT TOTAL:		667.82
4600-000	RENT	345681	8000	LM 5723	15/12/76	1,400.00
4700-000	LEGAL FEES	308823	6000	110576	05/11/76	1,100.00
4900-000	SALES TAX	308121	1000	SD 9923	01/11/76	37.92
		318723	1000	SD 9996	17/11/76	10.98
		345678	4000	7723	22/12/76	3.11
		345679	1000	SD 19823	25/12/76	18.82
		345682	2000	8823	23/12/76	2.95
				EXPENSE ACCOUNT TOTAL:		73.78
				GRAND TOTAL:		4,894.33

Figure 9.6

Before actually interfacing the Purchase Ledger Interface file to the Nominal Ledger, it is often useful to print a monthly 'Purchase Ledger/Nominal Ledger Distribution Cross Reference' report (Figure 9.6) showing distribution by account number of all new invoices entered for the month ended. The detail within each account may be suppressed, thereby showing only the total amount distributed to each Nominal Ledger account. Finally, a 'Vendor Analysis Report' can be produced at any time, showing the total amount billed, the number of invoices, and the average invoice amount for each vendor.

MANUAL PROCEDURES IN CHEQUE PROCESSING

A Purchase Ledger computer system, while simplifying cheque writing and reconciliation, does not remove all of the clerical burden. There are a number of points where extra care should be taken.

Firstly, when a computer prints a combined cheque and remittance advice it is possible that more than one advice-cheque will be required for a given payment. There may be several purchases from one vendor, resulting in a number of invoices to be paid. If this detail is too much to print on a single advice, the corresponding cheque is cancelled by the computer and the further invoice details continued on the next advice. This means that the cancelled cheque must be removed from the material sent to the vendor.

Secondly, the advice-cheques must be folded and inserted into envelopes for mailing. This process requires some forethought, since advice-cheques can be printed in three ways: the cheque beside the advice, the cheque following the advice, and the advice following the cheque. Side-by-side printing is often recommended because the computer can print both documents at the same time. However, this format is difficult to work with and does not save any appreciable time. The other two methods are more commonly used, especially if the advice-cheques are to be inserted into a window-faced envelope so that the name and address information will show. However, if automatic mailing equipment is to be used, then only the cheque printed first arrangement is suitable.

10 Sales Order Processing

INTRODUCTION

This chapter describes a computerised Order Processing system (or Order Entry system) and how it can improve customer service, reduce inventory holdings, and speed up the production of invoices. The system described is suitable for a distributing company, where supplies to stock are purchased from several manufacturers and orders for stock are from many customers. The typical Order Processing system serves four primary functions:

1. It provides order-filling information used by warehouse storemen to pick stock from inventory to be delivered to customers.
2. It updates computer inventory records based on incoming stock to inventory and filled orders despatched to customers.
3. It retains records of orders filled so that invoices can be produced once the goods have been delivered.
4. It retains summary data for accounting and sales analysis purposes as well as for predicting future inventory requirements.

Other activities, combined with these four, make the Order Processing system one of the more valuable as well as one of the more complex business computer applications.

Perhaps one of the most important considerations in a computerised Order Processing system is to ensure that the inventory records kept on the computer simulate the actual contents of the warehouse. Theoretically, if the inventory parts file held on the computer shows enough material on hand to fill an order, then enough material should be actually in the warehouse to send to a customer. This is certainly true theoretically, but in practice there are often discrepancies between the two figures. For example, storemen sometimes select incorrect stock, which means that too little stock is then available from the bin where the incorrect material was obtained. Similarly, when stock is received from goods inwards, it can sometimes be placed in the wrong bin. For these and other reasons (such as pilfering), the stock-on-hand figure on the inventory parts file does not always agree with the contents in the warehouse. However, the difference between the computer figure and what actually exists can be resolved by directly adjusting the computer figure whenever a discrepancy is discovered, and/or by adjusting the computer figure as a result of a periodic physical inventory of all stock. Suppose for example that the computer assigns 100 items of part number 12345 to a customer order. The computer inventory file shows an on-hand balance of 120 items, but the storeman finds only 90 items in the warehouse bin for part number 12345. It is then necessary to adjust both the customer's order to show the reduction in goods actually sent and also the inventory record to agree with the actual contents in the bin. A periodic physical inventory is another almost compulsory check to ensure that the computer figure is correct, and can be done continuously or as a regular stock-take of the whole warehouse.

INPUT TO THE SYSTEM

There are several types of input, other than adjustments to the stock-on-hand figure. The most familiar of these is the *customer order* which actually performs two functions. It provides information for filling the order plus information for updating the customer master file. The customer master file used is the same as that used in the Sales Ledger system. Orders can be received in a number of ways. The bulk of the orders usually arrive by post, but a certain percentage are telephoned or telexed. Where an order is telephoned or telexed, a standard order form may be used within the sales office to facilitate data entry. During order entry, an 'order number' is assigned to each order as it is entered. The customer number is verified and the customer name displayed. The responsible salesman and delivery address may automatically be pulled off the customer file, or manually entered. Any special delivery instructions can also be entered at this stage. Committed inventory is automatically controlled, and the facility exists to manually override prices. Each item on the order may be assigned a different discount percentage if necessary; and fully

SALES ORDER PROCESSING

141

interactive outstanding order control is provided. *Outstanding orders* are orders that cannot be filled because of insufficient stock. New stock must arrive before outstanding orders can be filled. Hence any unsatisfied balance of a customer order is placed on a special file called the outstanding orders file. Normally, satisfying outstanding orders is a high priority, and it is usual to attempt to fill them immediately after new stock has been received from the suppliers and inventory records updated. Thus *receipts of stock* (ie goods inwards) constitute another input to the system. Inventory receivings automatically update the average unit cost, selling price (if any price change), and quantity-on-hand on the Inventory file.

Another input to an order processing system is the *credit memo,* which is issued when goods are returned. It performs a dual function. So long as the goods can be resold, it is used to adjust the quantity-on-hand on the Inventory file. Secondly, it is also used to adjust the customer details. If the customer has not been invoiced for the goods, then it is a simple matter of adjusting the details of the original customer order which will still be on file. If however the customer has been invoiced, then the credit memo will need to act as an input to the Sales Ledger system, since invoice details are automatically interfaced with the Sales Ledger system. Thus the customer, in effect, gets a refund for the goods returned.

THE SYSTEM FILES

There are three main files in the order processing system:

— inventory master file;

— order details file;

— outstanding orders file.

The customer master file is not listed, as it is the same as that used in the Sales Ledger system. The inventory master file contains (per stock item) such details as: item number, description, product category, bin location, quantity-on-hand, outstanding order quantity (ie quantity committed), reorder level, unit of issue, unit selling price, average unit cost price, month-to-date and year-to-date sales and cost of sales figures, taxable status, quantity discount rate and discount quantity. There are two different types of discounts normally offered in an order processing system. *Quantity discounts* apply when a customer orders more than a given amount of a particular item. Details to enable quantity discounts to be calculated automatically are kept on the inventory master file. *Customer*

RUN DATE: 01-JAN-77　　　　　　　　　　　　　　　　　　　　　　　　　　　　　　　　　　PAGE 001
COMMISSIONS DUE REPORT

――SALESMAN――	――CUSTOMER――		――INVOICE――		
NO　NAME	NO　NAME	NO	DATE	AMOUNT	COMMISSION DUE
10　S. T. ROBINSON	10000　BETTER SERVICE CORP.	678901	28/12/76	4,419.69	220.99
		678902	29/12/76	920.40	46.02
		678905	30/12/76	261.90	13.10
		CUSTOMER TOTALS		5,601.99	280.11
	30000　XYZ MANUFACTURING CO.	678852	15/12/76	892.50	98.18
		678854	18/12/76	840.00	92.40
		CUSTOMER TOTALS		1,732.50	190.58
		SALESMAN TOTALS:		7,334.49	470.69

Figure 10.1

SALES ORDER PROCESSING

discounts apply to particular customers, and the details are kept on the customer master file. Cash discounts for prompt payment have not been mentioned here as they have been fully discussed in the chapter on the Sales Ledger system.

The order details file contains information about the order itself (order header), as well as information about each item on the order (item details). The order header (one per order) would typically contain: order number, order date, customer number, customer's purchase order number, delivery instructions, delivery address, etc. The item details (one per item) would contain such data as order number, item number, bin location, quantity ordered, quantity delivered, unit of issue, unit selling price, quantity discount rate (zero if no discount applicable).

The outstanding orders file also has one order header per order and as many item details as there are items outstanding. The order header would contain: order number, customer number, order date, customer's purchase order number, delivery instructions, etc. The item details would contain: order number, item number, quantity outstanding, quantity discount rate (only applicable if the *original* quantity ordered exceeded the discount quantity).

Output files from the system include:

— updated inventory master file;

— updated customer file;

— updated outstanding orders file;

— commissions due file;

— sales detail file;

— salesman file.

The commissions due file stores data on invoice totals and salesman responsible for use in the production of a 'Commissions Due Report' (Figure 10.1) showing total sales for each salesman number, and the corresponding commission due. The sales detail file contains invoice totals per customer for later interface to the Sales Ledger system. The salesman file simply contains the salesman number and name for each salesman.

RUN DATE: 01-JAN-77 PAGE 001
INVENTORY RECEIVINGS REPORT

ITEM NO	DESCRIPTN (1st 23 CHAR)	OLD ON-HD	QTY RCD	ORD CMP	NEW ON-HD	COST OLD-AVG	COST NEW-UNIT	COST NEW-AVG	PRICE-1 OLD	PRICE-1 NEW	PRICE-2 OLD	PRICE-2 NEW	PRICE-3 OLD	PRICE-3 NEW
CLMN 321	COLEMAN DOWNER SLEEPING	11	24	Y	35	11.000	11.000	11.000	21.95	21.95	20.00	20.00	18.00	18.00
TRLB 10001	TRAILBLAZER 10 × 7 AFRA	13	12	Y	25	35.000	39.000	36.920	69.95	79.95	60.00	70.00	50.00	60.00
VOIT 501	VOIT SWIM FLIPPERS - WO	35	24	Y	59	4.500	4.700	4.581	8.95	8.95	8.00	8.00	7.00	7.00

3 ENTRIES   TOTAL QTY RECEIVED: 60

Figure 10.2

RUN DATE: 01-JAN-77 PAGE 001
PURCHASING ADVICE REPORTS

ITEM NO	DESCRIPTION	AVERAGE COST	PRICE 1	PRICE 2	PRICE 3	QTY-ON HAND	REORD LEVEL	QTY-SOLD MTD	QTY-SOLD YTD	HIT-RO LEVEL	OUT STK
GRCA L-2000	GARCIA GAZ BUTANE LANTERN	5.400	10.79	9.50	8.00	41	50	199	401	X	
SYNWKS 176	SYNERGY WORKS SURVIVAL PARKA	56.000	99.00	90.00	80.00	0	10	21	226	X	X
TRLB 10001	TRAILBLAZER 10 × 7 AFRAME TENT	40.000	79.95	70.00	60.00	10	12	75	550	X	
VOIT 501	VOIT SWIM FLIPPERS - WOMENS	4.581	8.95	8.00	7.00	36	36	237	1,522	X	

4 ITEMS CHANGED STATUS

Figure 10.3

SALES ORDER PROCESSING

THE ORDER PROCESSING SYSTEM

Order header information is first entered into the system through visual display units and then each order item is entered (item number and quantity) and validated by reference to the inventory file. Stock is allocated on the stock record, whether it is available or not, thus ensuring that stock committed to outstanding orders is not available for subsequent orders. If stock is available, then order details are merged with any available outstanding orders from the outstanding orders file for the same customer. If stock is not available, then the order item details are written to the daily outstanding orders file. Those available items of the order plus any available outstanding items, are then sorted into bin location sequence and a copy of the order is then printed to act as a picking list for the storemen. The order details are then written to the order details file.

Once the goods have been picked, any amendments to the picking list are noted, and a video used to call up the relevant order so that the quantities can be revised. These changes automatically update the order details file, the inventory master file, and the daily outstanding orders file. The revised order is then used to print out a despatch note.

Goods inwards data is entered via a video, the inventory master file updated, and an 'Inventory Receivings Report' (Figure 10.2) printed. A 'Purchasing Advice Report' (Figure 10.3) is printed on request (usually daily) showing all items which fell below reorder level or went out of stock since the last printing of this report. Daily outstanding orders are merged with the outstanding orders file, the stock file consulted, and picking lists printed for those outstanding orders which have been available for some days. The reason for waiting a number of days is to see whether another order from that customer comes in during this waiting period, and if so, those available outstanding items can be added to the new order rather than print a picking list for only one or two items. In the event that this does not happen, then the above procedure is followed and such a small picking list printed.

Once the goods have been delivered, selected orders can be invoiced as and when required. Partial invoicing of an order is allowed, and adjustments to quantities delivered and quantities outstanding are still allowed even at this late stage. Miscellaneous charges, VAT, freight and any salesman commission amount or percentage due may also be entered at this time. The invoice names and addresses and customer discounts are retrieved from the customer file and a multipart invoice set produced (Figure 10.4).

INVOICE

		INVOICE	PAGe
		INVOICE	

SOLD TO: XXXXXXXXXXXXXXXXXXXXXXXX
XXXXXXXXXXXXXXXXXXXXXXXX
XXXXXXXXXXXXXXXXXXXXXXXX
XXXXXXXXXXXXXXXXXXXXXXXX

SHIP TO: XXXXXXXXXXXXXXXXXXXXXXXX
XXXXXXXXXXXXXXXXXXXXXXXX
XXXXXXXXXXXXXXXXXXXXXXXX
XXXXXXXXXXXXXXXXXXXXXXXX

ORDER =	ORDER DATE	CUSTOMER =	SALES MAN	PURCHASE ORDER =	SHIP VIA	COLL	PPD	TERMS
XXXXX	XX/XX/XX	XXXX	XX	XXXXXXXXXX	XXXXXXXXXXXXXXXX	X	X	XXXXXXXXXXXXXXXX

QTY ODERED	QTY SHIPPED	QTY BACK ORDERED	ITEM	DESCRIPTION	UNIT PRICE	DISK	EXTENDED PRICE
XXXX	XXXX	XXXX	XXXXXXXXXX	XXXXXXXXXXXXXXXXXXXXXXXXXXX	X,XXX.XX	XX	XXX,XXX.XX

COMMENTS
XXXXXXXXXXXXXXXXXXXXXXXXXXXXXXXXXXX
XXXXXXXXXXXXXXXXXXXXXXXXXXXXXXXXXXX

SALE AMOUNT	XXX,XXX.XX
MISC. CHARGES	XXX,XXX.XX
SALES TAX	XXX,XXX.XX
FREIGHT	XXX,XXX.XX
TOTAL	

Figure 10.4

SALES ORDER PROCESSING

Other miscellaneous management reports are also produced such as the 'Outstanding Order Report by Item', the 'Outstanding Order Report by Customer' (Figure 10.5), the 'Sales Analysis by Product Category' (Figure 10.6) as and when required. The sales analysis report shows sales, cost of sales, percentage of sales, profit and percentage of profit for each item within each category, both month-to-date and year-to-date, with a summary by category at the end.

POSSIBLE EXTENSIONS

The order processing system can be used for purposes other than to post inventory to customer orders. It can evaluate the location of parts within a warehouse; help detect pilferage or errors in picking orders; forecast future inventory needs; and automatically create purchase orders for suppliers. These four functions are not normally considered to be part of the order processing application. They are, however, a natural extension of it.

For bin location analysis, all that is necessary is for sales frequency statistics (the number of times an item is ordered) to be kept on the inventory master file. If the sales frequency is known, then it is possible to determine where best to locate items in the warehouse to increase order picking efficiency.

For pilferage detection, no additional information is required. All that is needed is for every discrepancy between the stock-on-hand figure on the inventory master file and the actual contents of the bin to be identified and reported. Such discrepancies can be caused by incorrect picking of stock; incorrect storage of new stock or returns; or loss of stock due to pilferage. A record should be maintained of all discrepancies, and an occasional analysis made of the resulting distribution. Any incidence of missing items which is higher than expected should trigger an immediate investigation.

Future inventory needs can again be determined more readily, if sales statistics are maintained. Inventory forecast and control is simply the name given to any system which provides management with sufficient information to enable them to retain only enough inventory to meet the demand for stock, to never run out of stock, and to allow economic lots of stock to be purchased. To be able to do this, more statistics on stock activity will need to be kept on the inventory master file. Such details as order frequency, average order quantity, quantity sold for each of the last

RUN DATE: 01-JAN-77   PAGE 001

OUTSTANDING ORDERS REPORT BY ITEM

ITEM NO	ITEM DESCRIPTION	CUSTOMER NO	CUSTOMER NAME	ORDER NO	ORDER DATE	QTY O/S	UNIT PRICE	DISC	CUSTOMERS P.O. NO
AMF 6773	AMF DELUXE SWIM MASK – LARGE	10000	BETTER SERVICE CORP.	123461	31/12/76	12	7.00	0	67623
		20000	ACMF DISTRIBUTORS, INC.	123459	12/12/76	4	7.50	10	AD 87232
		40000	NEIGHBORHOOD WOMEN'S CLUB	123460	30/12/76	3	7.95	0	NWC 767
		ITEM TOTALS:		3 ORDERS		19 = TOTAL O/S QTY THIS ITEM			
GRCA L-2000	GARCIA GAZ BUTANE LANTERN	10000	BETTER SERVICE CORP.	123461	31/12/76	7	8.00	0	67623
		ITEM TOTALS:		1 ORDERS		7 = TOTAL O/S QTY THIS ITEM			
SPLD 411	SUPERFLITE GOLF BALLS/3 PACK	20000	ACME DISTRIBUTORS, INC.	123459	29/12/76	60	2.75	10	AD 87232
		ITEM TOTALS:		1 ORDERS		60 = TOTAL O/S QTY THIS ITEM			
VOIT 501	VOIT SWIM FLIPPERS – WOMENS	40000	NEIGHBORHOOD WOMEN'S CLUB	123460	30/12/76	4	6.95	0	NWC 767
		ITEM TOTALS:		1 ORDERS		4 = TOTAL O/S QTY THIS ITEM			

RUN DATE: 01-JAN-77   PAGE 001

OUTSTANDING ORDERS REPORT BY CUSTOMER

CUSTOMER NO	CUSTOMER NAME	ITEM NO	ITEM DESCRIPTION	ORDER NO	ORDER DATE	QTY O/S	UNIT PRICE	DISC	CUSTOMERS P.O. NO
10000	BETTER SERVICE CORP.	AMF 6773	AMF DELUXE SWIM MASK – LARGE	123461	31/12/76	12	7.00	0	67623
		GRCA L-200	GARCIA GAZ BUTANE LANTERN	123461	31/12/76	7	8.00	0	67623
	CUSTOMER TOTALS:		2 ITEMS			19 = TOTAL O/S QTY THIS CUSTOMER			
20000	ACME DISTRIBUTORS, INC.	AMF 6773	AMF DELUXE SWIM MASK – LARGE	123459	29/12/76	4	7.50	10	AD 87232
		SPLD 411	SUPERFLITE GOLF BALLS/3 PACK	123459	29/12/76	60	2.75	10	AD 87232
	CUSTOMER TOTALS:		2 ITEMS			64 = TOTAL O/S QTY THIS CUSTOMER			
40000	NEIGHBORHOOD WOMEN'S CLUB	AMF 6773	AMF DELUXE SWIM MASK – LARGE	123460	30/12/76	3	7.95	0	NWC 767
		VOIT 501	VOIT SWIM FLIPPERS – WOMENS	123460	30/12/76	4	8.95	0	NWC 767
	CUSTOMER TOTALS:		2 ITEMS			7 = TOTAL O/S QTY THIS CUSTOMER			

Figure 10.5

SALES ORDER PROCESSING

twelve months, etc, will be needed as input into some reasonably sophisticated forecasting model. However, no matter how sophisticated the model is, it must always be remembered that a forecasting technique based on historical sales does not react quickly to a change in economic trends.

The last of the four additional functions, namely automatic creation of purchase orders, perhaps deserves the most comment. In the system described in this chapter, a 'Purchasing Advice Report' was produced showing all items which fell below reorder level or went out of stock. The purpose of such a report is to let the purchasing office know *when* to reorder a particular item. It does not indicate the *quantity* to be reordered. Nor does it say from whom the goods should be ordered. This is left up to the purchasing office. If however, the inventory master file was expanded to include (for each item) the supplier from whom that part is available and the reorder quantity, and also the supplier master file was on-line with average lead time figures, then it is possible to use the computer to actually print the purchase orders on pre-printed stationery. There are, however, both technical and behavioural reasons why a computer printed purchase order may not be feasible. One technical reason is that the supplier from whom a particular item is purchased may vary, or there may be several sources, depending on when and where the stock should be delivered. Even if the supplier does not vary, many unpredictable events such as strikes, fire, etc, could temporarily put a supplier out of action, thus requiring a change of supplier at the last minute. Alas, not all price concessions (such as quantity discounts) or demand conditions can be stored on the inventory master file. For instance a particularly hot summer or severe winter may place demands well above or below the forecasted seasonal fluctuations. This would mean that the computer calculated reorder quantity (economic reorder quantity) could be wildly inaccurate.

There are also behavioural reasons for not preparing purchase orders by computer. Purchasing officers or buyers invariably consider themselves ultimately responsible for purchase order decisions, and thus often feel it necessary to review computer printed purchase orders before they are mailed to the suppliers. This may be because they feel that computer forecasts for sales and computer calculated reorder quantities are questionable, or it may be because they know that no computer forecasting technique can possibly hope to handle all the factors which influence who should supply a particular item and how much. For example, if supplier

150 SMALL BUSINESS COMPUTERS FOR FIRST-TIME USERS

RUN DATE: 01-JAN-77 　　　　　　　　　　　　　　　　　　　　　　　　　　　　　　　　　　　　　　　PAGE 001
SALES ANALYSIS BY PRODUCT CATEGORY

CAT	ITEM- #	DESCRIPTION AVG-COST PRICE-1	PRICE-2	PRICE-3		QTY SOLD	COST-OF SALES	SALES	%-SALES OF-CAT	GROSS PROFIT	%-PROFIT OF-CAT
H	CLMN 321	COLEMAN DOWNER SLEEPING BAG 11.000　21.95　20.00		18.00	MTD: YTD:	42 352	462.00 3,072.00	756.00 5,536.00	7.06 9.09	294.00 2,464.00	7.53 10.58
H	GRCA L-200	GARCIA GAZ BUTANE LANTERN 5.400　10.79　9.50		8.00	MTD: YTD:	199 401	1,076.72 2,009.12	1,876.23 3,876.72	17.52 6.37	799.51 1,867.60	20.48 8.02
H	SYNWKS 176	SYNERGY WORKS SURVIVAL PARKA 56.000　99.00　90.00		80.00	MTD: YTD:	21 226	1,176.00 7,356.00	1,608.00 10,648.00	15.02 17.49	432.00 3,292.00	11.06 14.13
H	TRLB 10001	TRAILBLAZER 10 × 7 AFRAME TENT 36.920　79.95　70.00		60.00	MTD: YTD:	75 550	2,769.00 16,914.00	4,356.00 27,136.00	40.68 44.58	1,587.00 10,222.00	40.65 43.88
H	TRLR 10002	TRAILBLAZER BACK PACKER TENT 20.000　39.99　36.00		32.00	MTD: YTD:	66 496	1,320.00 8,220.00	2,112.00 13,672.00	19.72 22.46	792.00 5,452.00	20.28 23.40
	CATEGORY TOTALS:	5 ITEMS			MTD: YTD:	403 2,025	6,803.72 37,571.12	10,708.23 60,868.72	100.00 99.99	3,904.51 23,297.60	100.00 100.01

RUN DATE: 01-JAN-77 　　　　　　　　　　　　　　　　　　　　　　　　　　　　　　　　　　　　　　　PAGE 002
SUMMARY

PRD CAT	# ITM	COST-OF-SALES	MONTH-TO-DATE SALES	%-SALES	GROSS-PROFIT	%-PROFT	COST-OF-SALES	YEAR-TO-DATE SALES	%-SALES	GROSS-PROFIT	%-PROFIT
B	1	107.67	2,148.57	12.64	2,040.90	27.24	946.02	13,891.42	13.53	12,945.40	27.18
G	1	1,071.00	1,749.00	10.29	678.00	9.05	6,726.00	11,494.00	11.20	4,768.00	10.01
H	5	6,803.72	10,708.23	62.97	3,904.51	52.12	37,571.12	60,868.72	59.30	23,297.60	48.92
S	2	1,529.70	2,398.20	14.10	868.50	11.59	9,778.20	16,389.20	15.97	6,611.00	13.88
GRAND TOTALS: 4 CATEGORIES	9	9,512.09	17,004.00	100.00	7,491.91	100.00	55,021.34	102,643.34	100.00	47,622.00	99.99
CATEGORY AVERAGES:	2.2	2,378.02	4,251.00	25.00	1,872.98	25.00	13,755.34	25,660.84	25.00	11,905.50	25.00

Figure 10.6

SALES ORDER PROCESSING

lead time and demand for stock are two major factors, and it happens that either or both are subject to unpredictable fluctuations, then buyers may insist on adjusting computer calculated reorder quantities before the purchase order is printed. For these and other reasons, it may simply be more trouble than it is worth to print the purchase orders on the computer.

In spite of these technical and behavioural obstacles, preparing preprinted purchase orders by computer can sometimes be more efficient and less costly than preparing them by hand. If the source of stock is reasonably constant, and reorder quantities, average demand and supplier lead times can be accurately calculated, then a computer printed purchase order would save a considerable amount of typing time. This would leave the purchasing office with more time to devote to the less tedious tasks associated with purchasing, such as negotiating for better discounts, searching for new suppliers, etc.

11 Nominal Ledger

INTRODUCTION

The Nominal Ledger is a consolidated record of the balances of each of the accounts of a business and of the transactions to those accounts. The 'Chart of Accounts' is arranged to provide a means of classifying the transactions into meaningful categories for reporting and analysis. Transactions are usually posted to the Nominal Ledger on a periodic basis. This may be daily for a business with a very large volume of transactions and for a less active business it may be monthly or quarterly. Whatever the posting period, a Trial Balance must be taken upon completion of the posting to ensure that the Nominal Ledger is 'in balance'. It is a fundamental accounting principle that the Nominal Ledger must always be in balance; that is, the total of all accounts with debit balances must equal the total of all accounts with credit balances. The Trial Balance showing the beginning balance of each account, the transactions posted to it, and the resulting balance is periodically printed to prove that the Nominal Ledger balances. On a less frequent basis (usually quarterly or half-yearly), other financial statements such as a Balance Sheet or Profit and Loss Statement are prepared to give a picture of the business activities for the period.

The *Balance Sheet* reflects the financial position of the business at the close of business on the last day of the accounting period. It summarises all asset, liability and capital accounts. Its name is derived from the fundamental accounting equation:

$$ASSETS = LIABILITIES + CAPITAL$$

ie, total assets equal, or balance to, total liabilities plus total capital.

Assets are those items owned by the firm. Cash in the bank, accounts receivable, equipment and furniture are all assets. Total assets increase when additional equipment is purchased on credit; they decrease when payment on a pending invoice is made; or they remain constant when furniture is purchased with cash.

Assets come from resources contributed by two groups: the creditors and the owners. The creditors have supplied goods or services to the business and require payment in return. They have claim to the assets of the business for the amount owed to them. Their claims are termed 'liabilities'. Accounts payable, notes payable, and unearned income are liabilities. If equipment is bought on an instalment plan, assets are increased by the value of the equipment, but so are liabilities. The equipment is not completely owned by the business until the supplier has been fully paid.

The amount the owners invested in the business is called 'capital'. Capital is the margin of assets over liabilities and is sometimes called 'owner's equity'. Profits add to capital, whereas losses reduce it. The amount of capital should be a positive value; if not, the business is insolvent and likely to go into bankruptcy unless the owners invest more capital in the business. The *Profit and Loss Statement* reflects the operating results of a business over a period of time. It is composed of all income and all expense accounts.

The income comprises all sales revenues received by the business. Expenses include all costs incurred in generating sales and in operating the business. Salaries, advertising, rent, and utilities are all expenses generated by the business.

The final line of the Income Statement shows the remainder of income less expenses. If the business has had a favourable operating performance, the result is a profit (net income). However, if the expenses have been greater than the revenues, the result is a loss (net loss). The net income (or net loss) is entered into the capital section of the Balance Sheet to reflect the results of business operation for that period.

The Nominal Ledger is a truly integrated system. Several subsidiary accounting applications precede its development. The preparation of subsidiary Nominal Ledger files has been referred to several times throughout the descriptions of the various computer applications. Each subsidiary file summarises the detail for a particular application, such as Purchase Ledger, Sales Ledger, Payroll and Capital Assets. These sum-

NOMINAL LEDGER

mary totals are posted to the Nominal Ledger, and cross-referenced to permit tracing back to each subsidiary ledger. In other words, should a summary total be questioned, it must be possible to locate the figures that led to the questionable item. The cross-reference to a subsidiary ledger provides this audit trail. It is possible to isolate a transaction or a batch of transactions, such as a series of payroll cheques. The different levels of data accumulation – nominal ledger, subsidiary ledger, and batched transactions – reflect the hierarchy followed in a financial reporting system.

INPUT TO THE SYSTEM

A Nominal Ledger computer application may be almost completely designed as an extension of other computer applications. An examination of each computer application considered in previous chapters will show that summary data can be extracted for direct input into the Nominal Ledger application. In a Purchase Ledger computer application, for example, the original supplier invoices are recorded on the Purchase Ledger Voucher Register. This report shows details such as the voucher number, the supplier number and name, the invoice number, date and amount, the date the invoice is to be paid, plus the Nominal Ledger account numbers to which the invoice is to be distributed. This information is then summarised into a Distribution Cross-Reference report suitable for posting direct to the Nominal Ledger. The information on this Cross-Reference report is summarised and stored on an interface file for later posting to the Nominal Ledger.

Interface files from other computer applications supply other forms of input to the Nominal Ledger. For example:

— The Payroll computer application accumulates and totals such items as gross pay, tax withheld, voluntary deductions, etc. Each item subtotal is entered into a separate Nominal Ledger account.

— The Sales Ledger application provides two types of Nominal Ledger input. In this application a Monthly Sales Summary file and a Monthly Cash Receipts Summary file are created, both of which after suitable modification, can be used as input to the Nominal Ledger. For example, the cash Receipts Summary file must show both the actual cash amount received, and the amount of discount allowed before it can be used as input to the Nominal Ledger.

Collectively, the interface files from these subsidiary computer applications represent a massive amount of information that has been summarised into a form suitable for posting to the Nominal Ledger. These files supply the bulk of all entries to the ledger. Posting in this way represents obvious savings in human effort compared to the manual entry of summary totals.

However, it is also necessary to allow for the entry of additional ledger entries or corrections transferred from manually prepared journals. These are often called 'journal entries', and could include for example details of petty cash vouchers, handwritten cheques, etc. Considerably more detail (and authorisation) is expected for a journal entry than for data that is extracted from an existing computer application such as payroll. The reason for this is that the data passed on from a lower-level computer application such as payroll has already received considerable review, justification and authorisation, whereas the same is not true of a manual journal entry.

THE NOMINAL LEDGER SYSTEM

The Nominal Ledger system has two main files: the master file variously called the 'Nominal Ledger Master File' or 'Chart of Accounts File', and a Year-to-Date Transaction file.

Each record of the Chart of Accounts contains account number (eg. 7 digits; 4-digit main account number followed by a 3-digit sub-account number), account description, special codes for formatting the Financial Statements, account type (debit or credit), and up to 13 periods of budgeting and last year comparative information. The 3-digit sub-account may be used to designate 'profit centres'. The manually prepared journal entries and the summary interface files from other computer applications are the initial inputs to the system. Processing begins after the journal entries have been keyed in through a video onto a Transaction Work File. The data entered is: account number (with automatic verification and display of account description), date, debit/credit amount, source (a 3-character abbreviation for the document or system from which the transaction originated), and up to 30 characters of detailed reference. The interface files are also added directly to the Transaction Work File.

The main reason for introducing this intermediary step and creating a work file for new transactions is to ensure that the principle of 'double

NOMINAL LEDGER

RUN DATE: 01-JAN-77 NORTHWEST INDUSTRIES PTY LTD PAGE 001

NOMINAL LEDGER TRANSACTION REGISTER

NO	ACCOUNT DESCRIPTION	TRX DATE	DEBIT AMOUNT	CREDIT AMOUNT	SOURCE DOCUMENT	TRX REFERENCE
1030-000	CASH IN BANK – BARCLAYS	31/12/76	95,378.46		S/L	CASH RECEIPTS 1/12-31/12/76
1030-000	CASH IN BANK – BARCLAYS	31/12/76		1,152.56	GJ	EMPL PAID PR TAX 1/12-31/12/76
1030-000	CASH IN BANK – BARCLAYS	31/11/76		42,089.73	P/L	P/L PAID 1/12-31/12/76
1030-000	CASH IN BANK – BARCLAYS	31/12/76		19,701.85	GJ	TRANSFER TO LLOYDS ACCOUNT
1040-000	CASH IN BANK – LLOYDS	31/11/76		12,497.65	PR	PAYROLL 1/12-31/12/76
1040-000	CASH IN BANK – LLOYDS	31/11/76		7,204.20	GJ	PAYROLL TAX PAID 1/12-31/12/76
1040-000	CASH IN BANK – LLOYDS	31/12/76	19,701.85		GJ	TRANSFER FROM 1/12-31/12/76
1050-000	CASH IN BANK – MIDLAND	31/11/76		198.25	S/L	SALES TAX PAID 1/12-13/12/76
1070-000	ACCOUNTS RECEIVABLE	31/12/76	104,794.90		S/L	CASH RECEIPTS 1/12-31/12/76
1070-000	ACCOUNTS RECEIVABLE	31/12/76		95,378.46		
5170-000	SALES TAXES PAID	31/12/76	198.25		GJ	1/12-31/12/76
5180-000	TELEPHONE	31/12/76	801.76		P/L	1/12-31/12/76
5190-000	DEPRECIATION EXPENSE	31/12/76	3,828.91		GJ	DEPRECIATION 1/12-31/12/76
		TOTALS:	343,001.60	343,001.60		
14590000	HASH OF ACCOUNT #S					

48 ENTRIES

Figure 11.1

entry accounting' is observed. In a computer application this means that the main YTD Transaction File must be in balance. One way to ensure this is to insist that the Transaction Work File is in balance *before* it is merged with the YTD Transaction File. To assist in this, a Nominal Ledger Transaction Register (Figure 11.1) shows the details of all transactions on the Transaction Work File. This report can be scrutinized to ensure that the total of all credits is equal to the total of all debits. If this is not the case, then it usually means that one or more of the following errors were made during entry of the journal transactions into the computer:

— failure to post all transactions;
— failure to observe the principle of 'double entry accounting'. That is, if a transaction has the effect of increasing a debit account (eg cash at bank), then a corresponding increase must be made to a credit account (eg fees earned) or a decrease to a debit account (eg accounts receivable);
— posting a debit transaction as a credit and vice versa;
— posting the wrong amount of the transaction;
— posting the transaction to the wrong account.

Not all errors will be due to incorrect entry of the journal transactions. There may well be some errors in the summary data on the interface files, particularly in the areas of cash receipts and payroll. Whatever the cause of the errors, if the Transaction Work File is not in balance, then compensating corrections must be made to this file by means of further journal entries or changing those already on file. Once this work file is in balance, then it can be merged with the YTD Transaction File. This merged file then forms the hub of the Nominal Ledger system, and from it a host of output reports can be produced.

The first of these will undoubtedly be the 'Nominal Ledger Trial Balance' (Figure 11.2). It can be printed for any specified period by nominating starting and ending dates for transactions. This report shows the beginning balance, detailed credit and debit transactions, and ending balance for each account. At the operator's option, details may be omitted, thereby showing only summary figures for each account. It may also be printed for selected or all profit centres.

Perhaps the most important reports are the user formatted Financial Statements, including the Profit and Loss Statement (Figure 11.3), the

NOMINAL LEDGER 159

RUN DATE: 01-JAN-77 NORTHWEST INDUSTRIES PTY LTD. PAGE 001

NOMINAL LEDGER TRIAL BALANCE
FOR THE PERIOD 01/12/76 TO 31/12/76

ACCOUNT NO	DESCRIPTION	BEGINNING BALANCE	TRX DATE	SOURCE	DEBIT AMOUNT	CREDIT AMOUNT	NET-CHANGE	TRX-REFERENCE	ENDING-BAL
1030-000	CASH IN BANK – BARCLAYS	325,398.22	31/12/76	S/L	95,378.46			CASH RECEIPTS 1/12-31/12/76	
			31/12/76	GJ		1,152.56		EMPL PAID PR TAX 1/12-31/12/76	
			31/12/76	PP/L		42,089.73		P/L PAID 1/12-31/12/76	
			31/12/76	GJ		19,701.85		TRANSFER TO LLOYDS ACCOUNT	
			ACCT TOTALS:		95,378.46	62,944.14	32,434.32		357,832.54
1040-000	CASH IN BANK – LLOYDS	48,703.34	31/12/76	PR		12,497.65		PAYROLL 1/12-31/12/76	
			31/12/76	GJ		7,204.20		PAYROLL TAX PAID 1/12-31/12/76	
			31/12/76	GJ	19,701.85			TRANSFER FROM BARCLAYS ACCOUNT	
			ACCT TOTALS:		19,701.85	19,701.85	.00		48,703.34
1050-000	CASH IN BANK – MIDLAND	32,709.23	31/12/76	GJ		198.25		SALES TAX PAID 1/12-31/12/76	
			ACCT TOTALS:		.00	198.25	198.25CR		32,510.98
1060-000	PETTY CASH	1,998.87	(NO TRX THIS ACCOUNT)		.00	.00	.00		1,998.87
1070-000	ACCOUNTS RECEIVABLE	122,336.87	31/12/76	S/L	104,794.90			SALES 1/12-31/12/76	
			31/12/76	S/L		95,378.46		CASH RECEIPTS 1/12-31/12/76	
5170-000	SALES TAXES PAID	917.08	31/12/76	GJ	198.25			1/12-31/12/76	
			ACCT TOTALS:		198.25	.00	198.25		1,115.33
5180-000	TELEPHONE	3,708.87	31/12/76	P/L	801.76			1/12-31/12/76	
			ACCT TOTALS:		801.76	.00	801.76		4,510.63
5190-000	DEPRECIATION EXPENSE	17,712.03	31/12/76	GJ	3,828.91			DEPRECIATION 1/12-31/12/76	
			ACCT TOTALS:		3,828.91	.00	3,828.91		21,540.94
	GRAND TOTALS:	.00			343,001.60	343,001.60	.00		.00

Figure 11.2

Financial Reports may be printed without Budgets and Comparatives.
PAGE1

NORTHWEST INDUSTRIES PTY LTD
ALL DIVISIONS
UNAUDITED AND WITHOUT
OPINION EXPRESSED BY
J. SMITH (Accountant)

PROFIT AND LOSS STATEMENT
FOR THE PERIOD 01/12/76 TO 31/12/76

	CURRENT PERIOD RATIO	CURRENT PERIOD AMOUNT	YEAR TO DATE RATIO	YEAR TO DATE AMOUNT	BUDGETED CURRENT PERIOD RATIO	BUDGETED CURRENT PERIOD AMOUNT	BUDGETED YEAR TO DATE RATIO	BUDGETED YEAR TO DATE AMOUNT
SALES (SEE SALES SCHEDULE)	100.00	104,794.85	100.00	590,727.06	100.00	72,634.00	100.00	435,804.00
TOTAL SALES	100.00	104,794.85	100.00	590,727.06	100.00	72,634.00	100.00	435,804.00
COST OF SALES (SEE COST OF SALES SCHEDULE)	40.06	41,979.76	38.64	228,227.46	39.28	28,528.00	39.28	171,168.00
TOTAL COST OF SALES	40.06	41,979.76	38.64	228,227.46	39.28	28,528.00	39.28	171,168.00
GROSS PROFIT	59.94	62,815.09	61.36	362,499.60	60.72	44,106.00	60.72	264,636.00
OPERATING EXPENSES								
EXECUTIVE SALARIES	11.68	12,235.38	12.03	71,056.68	12.23	8,882.00	12.23	53,292.00
NON-EXEC WAGES	7.12	7,466.47	7.11	42,005.29	7.23	5,250.00	7.23	31,500.00
ADVERTISING	.99	1,034.14	.81	4,802.29	.83	600.00	.83	3,600.00
COMMISSIONS	.11	115.76	.11	651.26	.11	81.00	.11	486.00
HEAT, POWER & LIGHT	.50	525.04	.50	2,953.81	.51	369.00	.51	2,214.00
INSURANCE	.42	436.15	.47	2,792.64	.48	349.00	.48	2,094.00
LEGAL/ACCOUNTING	.39	404.61	.56	3,291.96	.57	411.00	.57	2,466.00
BANK CHARGES	.01	7.77	.01	43.72	.01	5.00	.01	30.00
OFFICE SUPPLIES	.30	310.93	.28	1,632.39	.28	204.00	.28	1,224.00
RENT	1.37	1,433.25	1.36	8,063.25	1.39	1,007.00	1.39	6,042.00
REPAIR & MAINTENANCE	.16	164.27	.16	924.17	.16	115.00	.16	690.00
EMPLOYER PAID PAYROLL TAXES	1.10	1,152.56	1.10	6,484.15	1.12	810.00	1.12	4,860.00
SALES TAXES PAID	.19	198.25	.19	1,115.33	.19	139.00	.19	834.00
TELEPHONE	.77	801.76	.76	4,510.63	.78	563.00	.78	3,378.00
DEPRECIATION EXPENSE	3.65	3,828.91	3.65	21,540.94	3.71	2,692.00	3.71	16,152.00
TOTAL EXPENSES	28.74	30,115.25	29.09	171,868.51	29.57	21,477.00	29.57	128,862.00
NET OPERATING INCOME	31.20	32,699.84	32.27	190,631.09	31.15	22,629.00	31.15	135,774.00
OTHER INCOME & EXPENSES								
TOTAL OTHER INC & EXP	.00	.00	.00	.00	.00	.00	.00	.00
NET INCOME (LOSS)	31.20	32,699.84	32.27	190,631.09	31.15	22,629.00	31.15	135,774.00

Figure 11.3

NOMINAL LEDGER

PAGE 1

NORTHWEST INDUSTRIES PTY LTD.
ALL DIVISIONS
UNAUDITED AND WITHOUT
OPINION EXPRESSED BY
J. SMITH (Accountant)

BALANCE SHEET

AS OF 31/12/76

ASSETS

CURRENT ASSETS			
CASH ON HAND		441,045.70	
(SEE CASH ON HAND SCHEDULE)			
ACCOUNTS RECEIVABLE	131,753.31		
ALLOWANCE – BAD DEBTS	(5,500.00)		
INVENTORY	295,091.17		
PREPAID EXPENSE	1,297.25	195,468.06	
TOTAL CURRENT ASSETS			863,687.46
PLANT, PROPERTY & EQUIPMENT			
OFFICE FURNITURE & FIXTURES	34,623.15	59,174.86	
VEHICLES	58,989.22	(4,125.00)	
MACHINERY	114,848.43	221,318.37	
ACCUMULATED DEPRECIATION	(72,503.60)	972.93	
(SEE DEPRECIATION SCHEDULE)			
			472,809.22
NET PROPERTY & EQUIPMENT		135,957.20	118,123.58
TOTAL ASSETS		999,644.66	590,932.80

Figure 11.4

PAGE 2

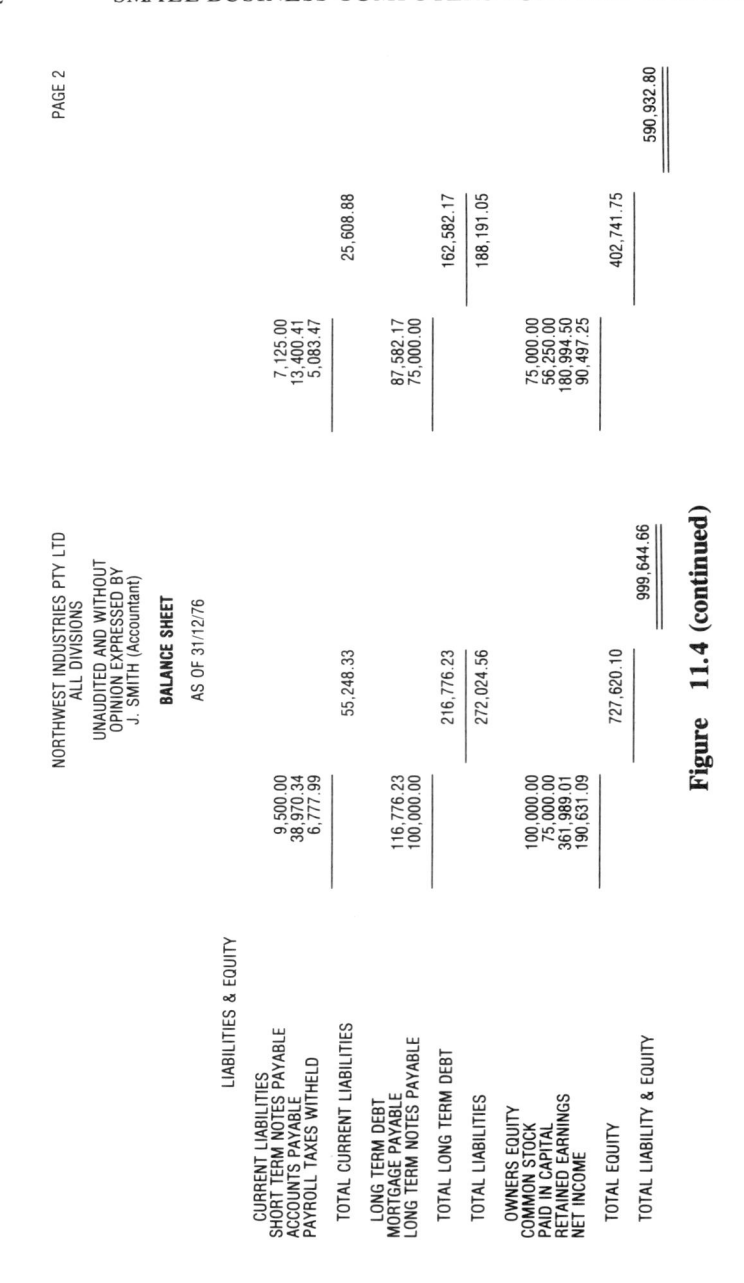

NORTHWEST INDUSTRIES PTY LTD
ALL DIVISIONS
UNAUDITED AND WITHOUT
OPINION EXPRESSED BY
J. SMITH (Accountant)

BALANCE SHEET

AS OF 31/12/76

LIABILITIES & EQUITY

CURRENT LIABILITIES			
SHORT TERM NOTES PAYABLE	9,500.00	7,125.00	
ACCOUNTS PAYABLE	38,970.34	13,400.41	
PAYROLL TAXES WITHELD	6,777.99	5,083.47	
TOTAL CURRENT LIABILITIES		55,248.33	25,608.88
LONG TERM DEBT			
MORTGAGE PAYABLE	116,776.23	87,582.17	
LONG TERM NOTES PAYABLE	100,000.00	75,000.00	
TOTAL LONG TERM DEBT		216,776.23	162,582.17
TOTAL LIABILITIES		272,024.56	188,191.05
OWNERS EQUITY			
COMMON STOCK	100,000.00	75,000.00	
PAID IN CAPITAL	75,000.00	56,250.00	
RETAINED EARNINGS	361,989.01	180,994.50	
NET INCOME	190,631.09	90,497.25	
TOTAL EQUITY		727,620.10	402,741.75
TOTAL LIABILITY & EQUITY		999,644.66	590,932.80

Figure 11.4 (continued)

NOMINAL LEDGER

Balance Sheet (Figure 11.4), and accompanying Supporting Schedules (Figures 11.5 and 11.6). The Financial Statement formatting codes provide considerable flexibility for these reports, allowing the user to structure them to suit his own requirements. The Financial Statements may be printed for any specified period and for selected or all profit centres. Optionally, budgets may be shown on the Profit and Loss Statement and last year comparatives on the Balance Sheet. Budgets or comparatives may also optionally be shown on the Supporting Schedules.

THE COMPANY CHART OF ACCOUNTS

Other special reports can be readily prepared if a company carefully plans its 'Chart of Accounts'. In a meaningful Chart of Accounts the first four digits of the account number may indicate the ledger entry function or purpose, and the last three digits subdivide the account number structure. Account XXXX-100, for example, might designate entries that apply to division or 'profit centre' one hundred. The first four digits make it possible, for example, to establish the total charge throughout all divisions for a particular type of expense.

The Chart of Accounts must be carefully designed and rigorously followed to permit new accounts to be added, and existing accounts to be restructured after it has been set up. Unfortunately, too many Charts of Accounts are designed when a company is small and there is little need to prepare detailed reports by separate account. As the firm grows, the Chart of Accounts evolves without a carefully considered system of classification. Consequently, more recent account numbers do not tie to older numbers in a meaningful way. It also frequently happens that an original Chart of Accounts was designed for a small business, and no provisions were made for additional company divisions. Account numbers are allowed to take on different meanings, depending on which division is using them.

Once a company begins to allow several Charts of Accounts to exist, several accounting systems must exist in parallel, at least to some degree. It is important therefore that a common consensus is reached between divisions of a company concerning the use of account numbers in their Chart of Accounts.

NORTHWEST INDUSTRIES PTY LTD
ALL DIVISIONS
UNAUDITED AND WITHOUT
OPINION EXPRESSED BY
J. SMITH (Accountant)

SALES SCHEDULE

FOR THE PERIOD 01/12/76 TO 31/12/76

PAGE 1

	CURRENT PERIOD		YEAR TO DATE		BUDGETED CURRENT PERIOD		BUDGETED YEAR TO DATE	
	RATIO	AMOUNT	RATIO	AMOUNT	RATIO	AMOUNT	RATIO	AMOUNT
SALES								
PRODUCT A SALES	72.65	76,128.82	72.89	430,567.27	72.44	52,616.00	72.44	315,696.00
PRODUCT B SALES	9.71	10,171.70	9.21	54,420.64	9.36	6,802.00	9.36	40,812.00
PRODUCT C SALES	15.20	15,924.76	15.45	91,283.08	15.71	11,410.00	15.71	68,460.00
PRODUCT D SALES	3.12	3,274.65	2.61	15,426.64	2.65	1,928.00	2.65	11,568.00
PRODUCT E SALES	.00	.00	.51	2,996.07	.51	374.00	.51	2,244.00
DISCOUNTS ALLOWED	1.25-	(1,310.02)	1.25-	(7,369.99)	1.27-	(921.00)	1.27-	(5,526.00)
FREIGHT OUT	.58	604.94	.58	3,403.35	.59	425.00	.59	2,550.00
TOTAL SALES	100.00	104,794.85	100.00	590,727.06	100.00	72,634.00	100.00	435,804.00

NORTHWEST INDUSTRIES PTY LTD
ALL DIVISIONS
UNAUDITED AND WITHOUT
OPINION EXPRESSED BY
J. SMITH (Accountant)

COST OF SALES SCHEDULE

FOR THE PERIOD 01/12/76 TO 31/12/76

PAGE 1

	CURRENT PERIOD		YEAR TO DATE		BUDGETED CURRENT PERIOD		BUDGETED YEAR TO DATE	
	RATIO	AMOUNT	RATIO	AMOUNT	RATIO	AMOUNT	RATIO	AMOUNT
COST OF SALES								
PURCHASES	31.55	33,062.37	30.14	178,059.58	30.64	22,257.00	30.64	133,542.00
PURCHASE DISCOUNTS	.41-	(427.45)	.41-	(2,404.81)	.41-	(300.00)	.41-	(1,800.00)
FREIGHT & SHIPPING	.30	317.32	.30	1,785.20	.31	223.00	.31	1,338.00
INVENTORY ADJUSTMENT	8.51	9,027.52	8.60	50,787.49	8.74	6,348.00	8.74	38,088.00
TOTAL COST OF SALES	40.06	41,979.76	38.64	228,227.46	39.28	28,528.00	39.28	171,168.00

Figure 11.5

NOMINAL LEDGER

NORTHWEST INDUSTRIES PTY LTD
ALL DIVISIONS
UNAUDITED AND WITHOUT
OPINION EXPRESSED BY
J. SMITH (Accountant)

CASH IN BANK SCHEDULE

AS OF 31/12/76   PAGE 1

CASH IN HAND	357,832.54	133,218.22
CASH IN BANK – BARCLAYS	48,703.34	35,510.96
CASH IN BANK – LLOYDS	32,510.98	25,219.73
CASH IN BANK – MIDLAND	1,998.87	1,499.15
PETTY CASH		
TOTAL CASH IN BANK	441,045.73	195,468.06

NORTHWEST INDUSTRIES PTY LTD
ALL DIVISIONS
UNAUDITED AND WITHOUT
OPINION EXPRESSED BY
J. SMITH (Accountant)

DEPRECIATION SCHEDULE

AS OF 31/12/76   PAGE 1

ACCUMULATED DEPRECIATION		
ACCUM DEPREC/FURNITURE	27,565.06	17,990.50
ACCUM DEPREC/VEHICLES	12,083.77	4,491.17
ACCUM DEPREC/MACHINERY	32,854.77	15,740.34
TOTAL DEPRECIATION	72,503.60	38,222.01

Figure 11.6

APPENDICES

1. Sample Study Questionnaires
2. Cost Elements of Computer Systems
3. Sample Study Report
4. Specimen Tender Document
5. Suggested Letter to Suppliers
6. Glossary of Terms

APPENDIX 1

Sample Study Questionnaires

1.1   Sales Order Processing
1.2   Invoicing
1.3   Sales Ledger
1.4   Purchase Ledger
1.5   Nominal Ledger
1.6   Payroll
1.7   Stock Control

1.1 SALES ORDER PROCESSING

1	No. of orders per week	–	(av and max)
2	Expected % of change per annum	–	(= %)
3	% details, if any, of daily, weekly seasonal variations	–	
4	No. of items per order	–	(av and max)
5	No. of outstanding orders	–	(av and max)
6	Special procedures, if any, for processing outstanding orders		
7	No. of returns from customers per week	–	(av and max)
8	No. of customers	–	(av and max)
9	Expected % of change per annum	–	(= %)
10	No. of customers with at least one delivery address different from account address	–	
11	From Q 10, no. of different delivery addresses per customer	–	(av and max)
12	% breakdown of how orders are received	–	
13	Details of variations in units of quantity	–	
14	Is immediate response required to customer enquiries?	–	
15	What are the type of enquiries?	–	
16	How many different units of measure exist in total?	–	
17	What is the maximum no. of units of measure that can apply to one item?	–	
18	What turnaround is required from receipt of order to despatch?	–	
19	How long are outstanding orders kept before action is taken?	–	
20	What are the maximum number of digits in each of the following?	–	
	Customer Identifier	–	
	Customer Order Number	–	
	Product Identifier	–	
	Quantity or Weight per item	–	
	Internal Order Number	–	
	Delivery Address	–	

1.2 INVOICING

1. No. of invoices produced per week — (av and max)
2. Expected % of change per annum — (= %)
3. No. of items on an invoice — (av and max)
4. Details of any seasonal variation —
5. Details of customer discount arrangements —
6. Details of any carriage and/or package charges —
7. Details of any separate invoicing arrangements —
8. Details of any variations in VAT rates across product lines —
9. What turnaround is required from receipt of order to despatch of invoice? —
10. Is immediate response required to enquiries regarding invoices? —
11. What are the types of enquiries?
12. Is VAT shown separately for each item? —
13. What are the maximum number of digits in each of the following? —
    - Customer Identifier —
    - Customer Order Number —
    - Invoice Address —
    - Product Identifier —
    - Quantity or Weight per item —
    - Unit price per item —
    - VAT value per item —
    - Extended goods value per item —
    - Total value per invoice —

1.3 SALES LEDGER

1. No. of accounts in Sales Ledger —
2. Expected % of change per annum — (= %)
3. No. of 'Live' accounts — (av and max)
4. Expected % change per annum — (= %)

SAMPLE STUDY QUESTIONNAIRES 173

5 If statements are produced then
     frequency of production   —
     average no. per month   —
     maximum no. per month   —
     expected % change per annum   — (= %)
6 Details of any ageing of the final balance   —
7 What is the outstanding debt?   —
8 What method of processing is required, open item or brought forward?   —
9 Is immediate response required to enquiries?   —
10 What is the nature of enquiries?   —
11 Details of any sales analyses required   —
12 What are the maximum number of digits in each of the following?
     Customer Identifier   —
     Customer Name   —
     Invoice Address   —
     Value of current month's invoices per customer   —
     Total outstanding balance per customer   —
     Sales value year-to-date per customer   —

1.4 PURCHASE LEDGER

1 No. of accounts in Purchase Ledger   —
2 Expected % change per annum   — (= %)
3 No. of 'Live' accounts   — av and max)
4 Expected % change per annum   — (= %)
5 No. of supplier's invoices received per week   —
6 Expected % change per annum   — (= %)
7 Details of any seasonal variations in Q5   —
8 No. of payments per month by:
     cheque   — (av and max)

	credit transfer	– (av and max)
	other methods	– (av and max)
9	Expected % change per annum in Q8	– (= %)
10	Details of seasonal variations in no. of payments and/or method of payment	–
11	What method of processing is required, open item or brought forward?	–
12	Details of any ageing of final balance	–
13	Is immediate response required to enquiries?	–
14	What is the nature of enquiries?	–
15	Details of any purchase analyses required	–
16	Details of any supplier discounts	–
17	What are the maximum no. of digits in each of following?	
	Supplier Identifier	–
	Supplier Name	–
	Supplier Address	–
	Account Balance	–
	Turnover for current month per supplier	–
	Turnover year-to-date per supplier	–
	No. of orders placed per year per supplier	–

1.5 NOMINAL LEDGER

1	No. of nominal ledger headings	–
2	Expected % change per annum	– (= %)
3	No. of postings to ledger per month	–
4	Expected % change per annum	– (= %)
5	No. of accounting periods per year	–
6	Is immediate response required to enquiries?	–
7	What is the nature of enquiries?	–
8	Details of any nominal analyses required	–

9 What are the maximum number of
   digits in each of the following?
      Nominal Heading Code   –
      Nominal Heading Description   –
      Current balance per heading   –
      Cumulative balance year-to-date   –
        per heading
      Budget value per heading   –
      Monthly account balance per   –
        heading

1.6 PAYROLL

1 No. of employees
      hourly paid   –
      weekly time rated   –
      weekly flat rated   –
      monthly salaried   –
2 Expected % change per annum in Q1   – (= %)
3 When does week finish?   –
4 When are earnings paid?   –
5 How is gross pay calculated per   –
   employee?
6 Details of deductions which can   –
   apply to each category of employee
7 Details of methods of payment for   –
   each category of employee
8 Is immediate response required to   –
   payroll enquiries?
9 What is the nature of enquiries?   –
10 Details of payroll analyses   –
   required and frequency
11 What are the maximum number of digits
   in each of the following?
      Employee No.   –
      Employee Name   –
      Hourly Rate per employee   –
      Bonus Rate per employee   –
      Overtime Rate per employee   –

Superannuation per employee —
Tax Code per employee —
N.H.I. deduction per employee —
Gross pay to date per employee —
Tax to date per employee —
Any other payment per employee —
Any other payment per employee (itemised) —
Any other deduction per employee (itemised) —

1.7 STOCK CONTROL

1. At what point are stocks held, eg finished, part-processed goods, raw materials —
2. At each main stock point what is
   Value of total stock? —
   No. of types of goods held? —
   No. of goods received per week? —
   No. of goods returned per week? —
   No. of goods issued per week?
3. Details of any seasonal peaks applying to any of Q2 —
4. Details of any advanced allocating of goods —
5. Details of which stock category is held under which heading, eg actual physical, allocated, free, on order —
6. Details of how up-to-date figures in various headings should be —
7. Details of variations in measures of goods —
8. Details of pricing methods —
9. Details of any quantity discounts —
10. Details of any minimum manufacturing and/or supplier's order quantities —
11. Details of goods coding system —
12. Details of any stock analyses required and frequency —

SAMPLE STUDY QUESTIONNAIRES 177

13 Details of setting of re-order   –
    levels and actual re-ordering
14 Is immediate response required to   –
    enquiries about stock?
15 What is the nature of enquiries?   –
16 What are the maximum number of
    digits in each of the following?
    Stock Code   –
    Item Description   –
    Quantity or weight of physical   –
        stock per item
    ditto allocated stock per item   –
    ditto free allocated stock per   –
        item
    ditto on order stock per item   –
    Re-order level   –
    Supplier's lead time per item   –
    Economic order quantity per item   –
    Supplier's minimum order   –
        quantity per item
    Cost price per item   –
    Selling price per item   –
    Discount   –
    VAT rate   –
    Supplier Code   –

APPENDIX 2

Cost Elements of Computer Systems

    2.1   Capital Costs
    2.2   Running Costs

COST ELEMENTS OF COMPUTER STUDIES 181

2.1 CAPITAL COSTS

Computer Equipment	– all items including CPU, VDUs, printer, storage devices, etc;
Software	– all system software including operating system, utilities, language compiler; applications packages, tailor-written programs;
Data Communications Equipment	– eg modems, acoustic couplers, line drivers;
Site Preparation	– Provision of clean power supply; air conditioning; flooring, partitioning;
Supplies	– desks for VDUs etc; data storage cabinets; fireproof storage media, eg disks or diskettes; stationery, both standard and special;
Implementation	– equipment delivery; documentation; training for management, operators and possibly programming;
Expansion	– extra hardware units and upgrades; additional applications software;
File Creation	– data collection and verification; data input and verification.

2.2 RUNNING COSTS

Staff	– any new staff specifically employed for the system; any marginal salaries due to upgrading existing staff for the system; any staff employed to replace operators, etc, in their old jobs;
Supplies	– consumables such as stationery, printer ribbons, etc;
Maintenance	– annual contract for maintenance and support of all hardware items; either support contract or contingency for software maintenance, support and updates;

Other costs — hardware insurance;
additional training.

NOTE:

Some capital costs especially for hardware and software may actually be annual costs if, for example, the hardware is rented or leased, and if the software is used under licence.

APPENDIX 3

Sample Study Report

THE ABC COMPANY LIMITED
COMPUTER FEASIBILITY STUDY

Prepared by:
A N OTHER   Date:

CONTENTS

1 Introduction
2 Background to the Study
3 Investigations
4 Future Requirements
5 Evaluation of Options
6 Recommendations
Appendix

SAMPLE STUDY REPORT

1 INTRODUCTION

1.1 Terms of Reference

The terms of reference for the study were agreed by the board of ABC and set out in a memorandum dated 1st October.

The purpose of the study was to determine the most cost-effective method of achieving the objectives laid down in the referenced memorandum. These objectives are detailed below.

The stated objectives of any future course of action were as follows:

a) Provide systems and procedures that will ensure the best possible level of customer service, eg immediate acknowledgement of orders and a target 24 hours between receipt of order and despatch.

b) Provide up-to-date, accurate information for management to enable them to maintain the level of service required.

c) Provide for the close monitoring and control of the financial performance of the company.

These objectives were seen to be inter-dependent and were thus to be viewed together.

The application areas to be considered were as follows:

— Sales Order Processing;

— Sales Invoicing;

— Sales Ledger;

— Purchase Order Monitoring;

— Purchase Ledger;

— Nominal Ledger;

— Stock Control;

— Payroll.

The study was to examine these areas separately and as a whole, to determine the possible methods of achieving the desired objectives. The likely costs and benefits of each method were to be assessed, and any other implications for staff and company procedures were to be identified.

1.2 Method

Each of the application areas was investigated in turn by discussions with the relevant departmental managers and other personnel. All the appropriate data was collected from each area and any problems and shortcomings with existing systems were noted.

In examining the possibility of using a computer system in the future, the advice and assistance of a professional computer consultant was used.

2 BACKGROUND TO THE STUDY

2.1 Original Problems

It was realised that over the last three years there has been a steady deterioration in the level of service given to our customers. This has been most noticeable in a number of areas particularly:

— delayed deliveries;

— slow generation of invoices.

This deterioration has coincided with a rapid growth in the turnover of the company, but it was felt that if the deterioration in service was allowed to continue then it could eventually adversely affect the growth, and lead to lower or zero growth in real terms.

Also, as a wholesaler and distributor of car accessories the company is in an extremely competitive business and any customers lost once could be lost forever. There was also the need, therefore, to maintain and preferably increase our competitive position.

2.2 The Problem Areas

It soon became evident that there was no single cause of the problems and, also, that many of the functional areas were affected. This is mainly due to the way in which all the areas are inter-dependent on one another both for the information they require and the information they produce. One prime example serves to illustrate this.

It was discovered that there was much obsolete stock being held in the stores, and that as a result there was not enough space for holding sufficient quantities of the right stock. This was due largely to the failure to match purchases with changing demand. As demand shifted to new lines there was no corresponding shift in the purchases from manufacturers, and thus less popular stock was being ordered in too large quantities.

A further result of this was that the relatively obsolete stock was not written down sufficiently thus giving an incomplete picture of profitability. Also, the tying up of money in slow or non-moving stock had an adverse effect on the cash flow.

However, underlying all these problems were a number of root causes. These were identified as follows:

a) Management information was not being provided quickly enough.

b) There was insufficient management information available in the right form, and readily accessible.

c) The existing manual procedures were too slow to cater for the level of business now being handled.

When assessing the current situation and some of the problems that had been identified it was decided that it was not sufficient to merely resolve the problems but that the opportunity would be taken to plan for the future by looking for a course of action that would mirror the long term policies of the company.

3 INVESTIGATIONS

All the application areas listed in 1.1 were investigated thoroughly, and the following sections summarise some of the problems involved, and the requirements necessary to meet the objectives. Some of the important data collected is summarised in the Appendix.

3.1 Sales Order Processing

Since this is where customers are serviced many of the problems are well known. Some of those identified are listed below:

a) Too few staff to handle the volume of orders.

b) Orders acknowledged and delivery dates given on the basis of erroneous information (six orders for the same line are all confirmed on the basis of the same stock value).

c) Up to two days can elapse before all the relevant documentation is produced, ie acknowledgements, picking lists and despatch notes.

d) The outstanding orders file is far too large, due to a) and b).

There are obviously other points but the above serve to indicate the sort of problems currently suffered and their impact. In terms of resolving these problems certain definite requirements were identified.

Specifically these were:

a) The capability of handling each day's orders within that day, together with any outstanding orders that can be processed and any relevant forward orders.

b) The ability to be able to respond to enquiries and quote delivery dates, preferably immediately.

These requirements can be exploded to indicate needs such as producing picking lists by midday and 3 pm but such details follow on logically from the above.

3.2 Sales Invoicing

At present invoices are produced and sent out without reference to the actual availability of the stock ordered. Thus out of stock items result in a credit note. There have been occasions where an entire order has been out of stock, and a credit note has been produced. In the future, it is felt that invoices should include all the picking list information annotated to indicate any items which are to follow.

3.3 Sales Ledger

There are currently few problems in handling the ledger but little use is made of the information for analysis purposes. This was felt to be a vital function of any future system as long as time and effort was available to extract and summarise the appropriate information.

3.4 Purchase Order Monitoring

Currently there is minimal recording of purchase order details making it difficult to progress outstanding orders and check for discrepancies and part-deliveries on receipt of the order. This would be a prerequisite in the future.

3.5 Purchase Ledger

The main comments regarding Purchasing are given in 3.4 and there are no other major problems at present in maintaining the purchase ledger.

SAMPLE STUDY REPORT

3.6 Nominal Ledger

There is currently a feeling that account headings could be reorganised to provide greater detail of information and, if further analyses are required in the future, this would certainly be necessary.

There are occasionally delays in posting transactions from the other ledgers but these are not significant in relation to the general delays in order processing.

3.7 Stock Control

Currently the two book system is used whereby the book containing the details of the previous day's issues and receipts is used to update the record cards whilst the second book is used for recording the current day's transactions. The roles are then reversed each day.

This unfortunately means that the cards contain the balance correct at the end of the previous day only, and so if many orders arrive for a popular line they could, in total, well exceed the stated balance. However, all orders are processed on the basis of the same balance leading to order delays in many cases.

This is the main problem with stock control at present, and the other shortcomings cited referred to what is not done at present. Two particular examples were the mechanism for re-ordering and the calculation of economic order quantities. At present these functions are carried out by the head storeman who uses his knowledge and experience to do the job. However, he is due to retire in 18 months time and so an alternative method will be needed.

The basic requirements resulting from the investigation were to maintain up to the minute figures of stockholdings and to formalise the stock valuations and re-ordering operations.

3.8 Payroll

There are no particular problems at present in this area, although if expansion in staffing levels continues, extra staff will be required in the wages office unless some form of automation is introduced.

4 FUTURE REQUIREMENTS

4.1 Introduction

When the objectives set out in section 2 are examined in the light of the results of the investigations, three main requirements result namely:

— the need for more up-to-date information;

— the need for more information;

— the need to speed up processing in some areas;

4.2 Up-to-Date Information

More up-to-date information is required in the Sales Order Processing area to ensure that any quotes to customers are based on accurate data.

It will also help to make Sales Invoicing more efficient and to reduce the problems of purchasing.

4.3 More Information

The need for more information is dictated mainly by the management of the various areas rather than the operations of those areas.

For example, the operation of the sales ledger would not benefit dramatically from more information, but management, by making use of further information extracted from the ledger, would be better able to monitor trends and react more quickly to them. Sufficient information, readily accessible and in a convenient form, is currently denied management.

4.4 Immediate Future

Whatever longer term measures are adopted, an essential prerequisite is seen to be the reorganisation and modernisation of the various systems and procedures used in the operational areas.

Many of the procedures have evolved over many years to cater for new situations that have arisen. They have been modified and added to continuously to the extent that, if it were not for the long serving experienced personnel in many areas, eg stores, a situation of chaos would quickly result.

The value of such personnel should be acknowledged but the dangers

SAMPLE STUDY REPORT

to the long term viability of the company should be noted, especially with cases of prolonged illness or retirement.

Thus, the first requirement is for the detailed examination of all procedures and, where necessary, the re-designing of the procedures so that they mirror the current level and nature of operations and also take account of the future, ie they must be robust.

4.5 Options for the Future

The requirement detailed in 4.3 should go some way towards improving the immediacy and quality of information. But not the whole way.

Two major alternatives are seen for the company if the stated objectives are to be met:

— to increase staffing levels considerably in crucial areas;

— to use a modern digital computer system.

The costs and benefits associated with these options are discussed in the next section.

5 EVALUATION OF OPTIONS

5.1 Increasing Staffing Levels

5.1.1 Costs

It has been estimated that an increase of around 20 clerical and supervisory staff would be required, almost immediately, to improve the throughput of orders and organise and prepare information.

If a cost of £3,500 per annum is taken as average, then at current levels of cost, £350,000 would be required over five years to meet this increase.

However, there are other intangible costs which may be involved. Firstly, depending on the degree of expansion of company business then staff increases may be necessary to cope with the level of business. Secondly, staff increases tend to be relatively permanent and once levels have been increased they can often only be reduced through natural wastage.

5.1.2 Benefits

The benefits with this approach are difficult to assess in quantitative terms and so the view was taken that the possible achievement of the objectives should be examined and commented upon.

With greater staffing levels the sheer volume of orders should be processed adequately within the target lead times.

However, the maintenance and provision of up-to-date information could prove to be more difficult. Despite rigorous controls and discipline, human errors can still occur and thus the maintenance of information alone may be less than satisfactory.

The provision of information in a usable form will require a considerable amount of time and effort since it will involve the regular collection, collation and presentation of information for management. The magnitude of such tasks should not be underestimated.

5.2 Computer System

5.2.1 Type of System

There are two basic types of computer system that could be considered, namely the use of a computer bureau or the acquisition of our own in-house computer system.

There are advantages to be gained from using a bureau especially in terms of support, both for the initial phases of operation and for future changes and resilience to problems. However, other considerations from ABC's point of view weighed heavily against using a bureau: specifically the concept of shared resources and the potential for conflicts of priorities; the use of BT data communications facilities which could introduce a further failure point into the system; finally the costs involved are on-going for the life of the system.

Thus, together with the flexibility offered by an in-house system it was decided that our own system should be favoured. However, to ensure that there was no arbitrary element to the decision, a sample quote was requested from a bureau. This is noted in 5.2.2.

Taking the acquisition of an in-house computer system as the preferable option, the expertise of a computer specialist was used first of all to size the system and then estimate the likely costs involved.

The objectives and requirements set out earlier dictate that an on-line computer system is required. On-line means that files of data and prog-

SAMPLE STUDY REPORT

rams are available at all times for immediate access and use. There are two main types of on-line systems. The first concerns on-line interrogation. This means that information is given on demand but the physical contents of the computer record remain unchanged. For example, a stock enquiry would display information about a particular line but the volumes shown on the display would not be amended.

The second type of on-line system is concerned with on-line update (sometimes called interactive or real-time). With this type of system, the contents of the computer record can be changed via a terminal immediately; for example, the allocation of payments against a purchase ledger or the reduction or reservation of stock. It should be noted that on-line update involves more complicated recovery in terms of corruption of data.

For the purposes of ABC it was felt that the on-line update system would be required to cater for the sales order processing and stock control requirements alone.

A likely system would comprise three Visual Display Units in the sales office, one in accounts, and one in stores. The units in the sales office could be used for enquiring about stock levels so as to confirm orders and give delivery dates, and also generate picking lists, despatch notes and the allocation of future stock. Current outstanding orders could also be called up and processed along with new orders.

The accounts office VDU terminal would be used for ledger postings, account enquiries and to generate sales, purchase and nominal analyses when required. The VDU in stores would be used to update stock records immediately upon receipt or issue of any item, and also to produce stock checklists and so forth.

It is likely that the actual computer and printer would be sited in the accounts office since it is conveniently sited close to the stores and to despatch for the distribution of picking lists and despatch notes. Also the management reports required could be requested and produced in the one place.

Computer *software* can take the form of software packages. These will probably be in use by other organisations but some tailoring to the packages or additions to the packages could be required to suit our requirements. Alternatively, the software could be written specifically to our requirements.

Because of the need to re-examine our procedures as a prerequisite to any new system, it was felt that we could be flexible in our approach to software packages and the facilities they offered. They are favoured on the whole because:

— they are tried, tested and thus fairly reliable;

— they are cheaper than custom software.

It may well be that some modifications would be required, but for costing purposes the straightforward adoption of existing packages was assumed.

5.2.2 Costs

The basic costs refer to the *capital costs* of acquiring a computer system and *recurring costs* of running that system.

The equipment likely to be required is as follows:

— Central Processing Unit (CPU) of sufficient size to run several programs simultaneously;

— 5 Visual Display Units (VDUs) – 3 for sales, 1 for stores and 1 for accounts;

— printer;

— disk storage of up to 20M characters.

The cost of this equipment would be in the region of £35,000-40,000.

The cost of the software packages to handle the applications set out in section 1 could be about £11,000. There would also be costs associated with the system software. This is the software that controls the computer and gives various facilities such as file copy, sort and interrogation. A sample cost for this is £2,000.

There are many other possible costs that could be involved, but the main ones that will contribute significantly to the costs are those above. For example, a delivery charge of £400 could be involved and staff training costs of £1,000 could be noted.

The *running costs* will involve the maintenance and insurance of the system and the employment of a computer specialist. These costs are likely to be (per annum):

SAMPLE STUDY REPORT

Maintenance	£3,500-£4,000
Insurance	300
Staff	£6,000

Thus the total costs of the system over a five year period would be in the region of £102,000.

By way of comparison an estimate was given by a computer bureau, based on the volumes of data and transactions recorded and this was £25,000-30,000 per annum.

There are not felt to be any *other significant costs*. Most of the staff interviewed during the course of the investigations were enthusiastic about the idea of a computer system and it is likely that a system would receive their full support.

5.2.3 Benefits

The main benefits of a computer are felt to be that it could achieve all the objectives set out in 2.3.

To offset against the costs there are a number of potential savings that have been identified.

— Reduction in Capital Expenditure on typewriters, copiers, etc. This equipment will need replacing in 2-3 years' time at an estimated cost of £15,000.

— Reduction in interest on stock by increased stock turnover. A 10% reduction in stock holding should be possible while still maintaining service levels. Assuming a finance charge for stock of 20% per annum this would release a total of £80,000 over 5 years.

— Reduction in staff. It should be possible to save two staff due to automatic production of invoices and picking documentation. Over a five year period this should save £35,000.

As a conservative estimate the total savings over 5 years are:

Equipment	—	£15,000
Interest on stock	—	£80,000
Staff	—	£35,000
Total	—	£130,000

A computer could also provide the capability for expansion of the company's business without the need for additional clerical staff.

5.2.4 Other Considerations

There are unlikely to be significant problems encountered on the personnel and organisational side. Firstly, as noted above, most staff are enthusiastic and thus resistance should be minimal, if there is any at all. Secondly, there will be few job losses, merely control of the increase in staff, and thirdly with many of the tedious repetitive elements of work being taken over by the computer, job satisfaction could well increase.

Also, because of the need for procedural reorganisations anyway, any extra reorganisation due to a computer is likely to be beneficial.

However, it is as well to be aware of the implementation aspects of a computer system. Computers are not installed and become operational overnight. Up to 2 years could elapse before a system is fully working in all the application areas of interest.

A great deal of time, effort and involvement would be necessary from all concerned and the availability of staff must therefore be borne in mind. This is particularly important when one considers that normal day-to-day activities must continue whilst a computer is being installed.

6 RECOMMENDATIONS

The three comparative five-year costs are:

Non-computer solution	– £350,000
Bureau computer	– £137,000
In-house computer	– £102,000

With these costs and the possible benefits in mind it is recommended that a small disk-based computer system be acquired by the company.

When one appreciates that such computer systems are capable of being operated by existing office staff, are becoming relatively cheaper, and, with careful selection, should be capable of expanding to match any company growth, then the in-house computer system appears to provide the most cost-effective solution to the problems of meeting the company's objectives.

The second recommendation, therefore, is that a statement of our data

SAMPLE STUDY REPORT

processing requirements be prepared as a tender document and suppliers' proposals be requested.

APPENDIX

SUMMARY OF VOLUMES IN EXISTING SYSTEMS

Number of Orders/month – post	1400 av	2800 max
Number of Orders/month – other	600 av	1200 max
Number of Items/order	3 av	30 max
Telephone Enquiries/month	500 av	1000 max
Outstanding Orders/month	1000 av	3500 max
Number of Characters/order	70 av	420 max
Number of Sales Invoices/month	5000 av	10000 max
Number of lines/invoice	3 av	30 max
Number of returns from customers/month	100 av	250 max
Number of Customer accounts	2500	
Number of Statements/month	1800	
Number of Representatives	25	
Number of Supplier Accounts	510	
Number of Purchase Orders/month	600 av	1000 max
Number of Purchase Invoices/month	1000 av	1500 max
Number of Payments/month	100 av	
Number of Nominal accounts	270	
Number of Nominal Postings/month	500 av	
Number of Stock Items	2000	
Number of Issues or Receipts/month	30,000 av	
Number of Price Changes/month	10 min	1000 max
Number of hourly paid employees	120	
Number of weekly paid employees	30	
Number of monthly paid employees	30	

Note:
If part deliveries are involved due either to out-of-stock or physically large orders, then separate invoices are produced. The average is 2-3 invoices per order.

APPENDIX 4

Specimen Tender Document

THE ABC COMPANY LIMITED
DATA PROCESSING REQUIREMENTS

Prepared by:
A N Other
The ABC Company Limited
Street Lane
East Chester
E1 8XY
Tel: 071-623 2345   Date:

THE ABC COMPANY LIMITED
DATA PROCESSING REQUIREMENTS

CONTENTS

1 Introduction
2 Computer Applications
3 Suppliers' Proposals
Appendices

SPECIMEN TENDER DOCUMENT 201

1 INTRODUCTION

1.1 Background

Following a Computer Feasibility Study, the ABC Company Limited (subsequently referred to as ABC) are now inviting computer manufacturers/software houses to submit proposals to fulfil the data processing requirements outlined in this report.

1.2 The Company

ABC, founded over 70 years ago, is a wholesaler and distributor of a selected range of motor-car accessories. Current turnover is approximately £3million and the company expects to increase the amount of business by three times in the next five years.

The company deals almost exclusively with account customers only. All items carried are described in the ABC catalogue and are identified by a list number, which the customer uses to order an item. Certain list items are composed of more than one assembly item which are uniquely identified in the stores.

1.3 Purpose of the Report

This report is the document upon which suppliers are asked to base their proposals.

General information about the proposed computer based systems is provided, so that the type of equipment configuration can be determined.

Outline descriptions of each unit of the proposed system are given so that a quotation may be prepared for the detail system design work, programming, testing and implementation.

Section 3 shows the structure which the proposals should take and the information they should contain.

Although both Section 2 and the Appendices are broken down into a number of units or subsystems, this is for convenience of specification only and the solution to be aimed for is a fully integrated system.

Initially, ABC wishes to minimise its own staff involvement in systems design and programming.

It is intended that a single contract is placed for both equipment and software. It is, however, appreciated that a computer manufacturer and a separate software house may be required. Should this be the case, the leading organisation should prepare the proposal giving details of any other organisations who may be employed as sub-contractors for providing the equipment, systems design or programming. The leading organisation should ideally take contract responsibility for the system as a whole.

2 COMPUTER APPLICATIONS

2.1 General

The following paragraphs describe briefly the applications which it is intended to implement, more detailed information on volumes and field sizes is contained in the Appendices as a guide to file sizing. Implementation of the computer systems is to be phased; taking the Ledger Applications first, followed by the Sales Order Processing/Stock Control/Sales Invoicing. The Payroll and Purchase Order Monitoring will probably be the last applications to be phased in.

2.2 Sales Order Processing (see Appendix A1)

The system should cater for the direct input and validation of sales orders. Most orders are received through the post; the system must, however, cater for the input of orders taken on the telephone and be readily available to provide answers to telephone sales enquiries.

The system should be able to handle forward orders since some customers place a schedule of advance orders with ABC.

Picking lists are to be printed in the warehouse as each order is input. Once all items on a picking list which are physically on the shelves have been picked, details of the quantities actually ready for despatch and any carriage and packing charges are to be input to the system in the warehouse. If these details are not input to the system within a fixed time period a report of unreleased picking lists should be produced. Part orders are to be despatched, either if an out-of-stock position is discovered as a result of processing the initial order or if an out-of-stock is identified in the warehouse even though the item appeared on the picking list. Advice notes will be printed showing items which are to follow. The system must, however, cater for certain exceptional circumstances when, for instance, either an entire order or certain items on an order must be held because of an out-of-stock position. This situation may arise when a customer has ordered, for instance, two items, one of which cannot be despatched without the other, or when a customer has placed a high value order and only a low cost item could be despatched. Details of any items on a customer's order which cannot be despatched should be retained on an outstanding orders file. This file should be available for on-line interrogation to answer any customer queries. Whenever goods are received into stock the outstanding orders should be automatically reviewed and where possible released in priority sequence. The default priority should be derived from date of receipt of order but could be overridden by a management decision.

The system should be capable of accepting amendments to and deletions from existing customers' orders held at either the order processing stage or on the outstanding or forward order files.

For reporting purposes, orders should be associated with the originator, whether company representative, telephoned order or order received by the post. A history file of customer order details should be maintained for up to three months for enquiry purposes. The file details should then be printed for reference purposes.

The system should be able to provide a credit check for each customer and should also provide on request a report detailing the value of orders outstanding.

2.3 Sales Invoicing (see Appendix A2)

Invoices should repeat all the information on the advice notes, with the price of each item, VAT and customer discount having been applied automatically by the system. Any carriage and packing charges will also appear on the invoice.

Credit notes should be automatically produced where necessary and accounted for.

Export invoices should be highlighted by the system. Invoice details should finally be retained by the system for subsequent automatic posting to the sales ledger.

2.4 Stock Recording and Control (see Appendix A3)

The system should automatically maintain details of each stocked item.

Economic re-order quantities and re-order levels should be calculated automatically.

Both physical and free stock quantities should be maintained. When a low free stock position is encountered, this should be reported; similarly when free stock reaches zero this should be reported.

A stock list should be produced for valuation purposes and a stock checklist should be produced for stocktaking, which could in turn result in production of a stock discrepancy list.

A routine should be provided to be used on request for monitoring selling prices. This routine should calculate a suggested selling price for each item by applying a given mark-up factor to the latest buying-in price sufficient to cover the maximum customer discount and print out the result. The system should retain the cost price and date of receipt for physical stock purchased at different times.

Cumulative demand over the last four months should be available for each item by home or export sale. The cumulative annual value of demand for each item should also be available for each item.

For each item, the final stock position should be available and a stock history file maintained to identify the transactions which have gone to make up this position.

2.5 Sales Ledger and Sales Analysis (see Appendix A4)

A sales ledger file should be automatically maintained on an open-item basis and customer statements should be produced monthly.

An aged debt report (ageing the last three months separately and cumulative over three months) should be produced. A listing of overdue accounts is required giving the telephone and telex numbers (where applicable) of the customer to assist in the chasing of bad debts.

Each month a representatives' commission report should be produced, giving by invoice number, the value (exclusive of VAT) of each item on the invoice.

This subsystem should provide automatic input to update the nominal ledger.

2.6 Purchase Order Monitoring (see Appendix A5)

The system should maintain a file of outstanding purchase orders. This file should be available to check the original purchase order price with the purchase invoice value once the invoice is received. Any discrepancies should automatically be highlighted for manual correction.

Upon request a report showing the value of purchase orders for which an invoice has not been received should be available.

This subsystem should provide automatic input to update the purchase ledger.

2.7 Purchase Ledger and Purchase Analyses (see Appendix A6)

A purchase ledger file should be automatically maintained on an open-time basis. The system should produce remittance advices and a payments list.

This subsystem should provide automatic input to update the nominal ledger.

2.8 Nominal Ledger (see Appendix A7)

The system should maintain the nominal ledger as a result of bringing together the transactions created from the sales and purchase ledger systems. Other transaction information will be introduced into the system in respect of non-computer generated transactions.

A requirement also exists to input annual budgets for each account code and produce a monthly budget comparisons report.

2.9 Payroll (see Appendix A8)

The system should produce payslips for the hourly-paid employees from the clock-card details. Payslips should also be produced for the weekly and monthly salaried employees. The hourly paid and weekly salaried employees are paid cash whereas the monthly salaried are paid by credit transfer.

3 SUPPLIERS' PROPOSALS

The proposal should contain the following information and relate closely to the headings specfied. A standard approach is necessary in order to simplify evaluation and ensure that each proposal meets the requirements specified.

3.1 Introduction and Summary of Proposal

A summary page should be given listing the equipment proposed and overall costs for the hardware, maintenance, applications software and system software.

3.2 Recommended Equipment

The following information should be given:

— details of the operating characteristics of each item of equipment showing costs for purchase and rental;

— the capability for expanding the configuration;

— the mode of degradation in the event of power failure.

3.3 Software

This should give details of all items of software with costs where relevant, which the company would be likely to use or which could be required to operate the equipment and systems. It should give the following information where applicable.

3.3.1 Overall Picture

Concise description of proposed systems showing, in particular, any system integration.

3.3.2 Applications Packages

— basic concepts;

— policy on amendments/additions;

— ownership;

— statutory changes, program maintenance;

— guarantee period.

3.3.3 Tailored Systems

— precise definition of services offered;

SPECIMEN TENDER DOCUMENT

- software responsibility, sub-contractor policy and overall responsibility;
- calibre and experience of staff; for software houses, the period for which the software house has been in existence and number of staff;
- program maintenance responsibility;
- error notification and response procedure;
- guarantee or acceptance period.

3.3.4 *System Software*

- operating system functions;
- age of particular operating system and number of users of version specified;
- maintenance and enhancement policy;
- utilities;
- systems and programming aids;
- recommended language;
- other possible languages;
- report generation software;
- screen format generation method;
- ad hoc enquiry facilities;
- communications.

3.4 Support

The support which can be provided should be itemised including costs where relevant. The following information should be given:

- account responsibility;
- training facilities and costs (systems/installation and programming);
- time required for scheduled maintenance;

- response time to called-out maintenance;
- the location of staff for maintenance cover and the cost of called-out and on-call services;
- the extent and nature of back-up services in the event of prolonged machine failure;
- any other support available.

3.5 General

- installation requirements and related costs;
- the nature of systems documentation provided;
- recommended implementation procedure and plan;
- delivery date;
- insurance and delivery costs;
- costs of ancillary supplies(disk packs, paper, etc);
- names and addresses of companies and persons for organisations operating similar applications and using similar equipment to whom reference may be made;
- number of UK users of proposed model;
- number of UK users of the standard software;
- list of local users;
- copies of suppliers' standard contract terms covering rental, purchase, maintenance and supply of software or services.

APPENDICES

A1   Sales Order Processing
A2   Sales Invoicing
A3   Stock Recording and Control
A4   Sales Ledger and Sales Analysis
A5   Purchase Order Monitoring
A6   Purchase Ledger and Purchase Analysis

SPECIMEN TENDER DOCUMENT

A7   Nominal Ledger
A8   Payroll

Note:

The file sizes are only given as a guide; additional storage will be required for the software, transaction data, sort files, etc, and allowance must be made for file indexes and any blocking of data.

APPENDIX 5

Suggested Letter to Suppliers

Dear....................

I enclose an outline Statement of Data Processing Requirements presented on behalf of the ABC Company Limited.

I should be grateful if you would confirm that you are interested in submitting a proposal and that it will be available by the
....

Any queries regarding the content of the report and the requirements of the ABC Company Limited should be directed to myself.

........................copies of the proposal are required by the above date.

I look forward to hearing from you further.

Yours ....

Enc.

FORMS

Title	System	Document	Name	Sheet
SALES ORDER PROCESSING			THE ABC COMPANY LIMITED	A1.1

Inputs

    Customer Orders
    Forward Orders
    New Customers/Deletions/Amendments
    Release of/Changes to Picking Lists
    Carriage and Packing Charges

Processes

    Update Stock File
    Maintain Forward Orders File
    Update Customer File
    Create Invoice Suspense File
    Update Order History File
    Prepare Picking Lists
    Prepare Advice Notes
    Prepare Source of Sale Analysis
    Prepare Unreleased Picking List Report
    Prepare Order History Report
    Prepare Value of Outstanding Orders Report

Files

    Stock
    Outstanding Orders
    Customer
    Forward Order
    Invoice Suspense
    (to Sales Invoicing)
    Order History

Outputs

    Picking Lists
    Advice Notes
    Source of Sale Analysis
    Unreleased Picking List Report
    Order History Report
    Value of Outstanding Orders Report

Notes, cross-references

SALES ORDER PROCESSING **THE ABC COMPANY LTD** A1.2

VOLUMES

Number of orders per month	post	1,400 ave	2,800 max
	telephone	600 ave	1,200 max
Number of items per order:		3 ave	30 max
Telephone enquiries per month:		500 ave	1,000 max
Outstanding orders per month:		1,000 ave	3,500 max

FORMS

SALES ORDER PROCESSING   **THE ABC COMPANY LTD**   A1.3

OUTSTANDING ORDER/ORDER HISTORY RECORDS

Customer account number	9(8)	
ABC order number	9(6)	
Customer order number	9(6)	
Date	9(6)	DDMMYY
Source of sale identifier	9(1)	
Rep code (where applicable)	9(3)	
Product code) repeated for required	9(8)	
Quantity) number of items	9(5)	

RECORD SIZE: Approx 70 characters

FORMS

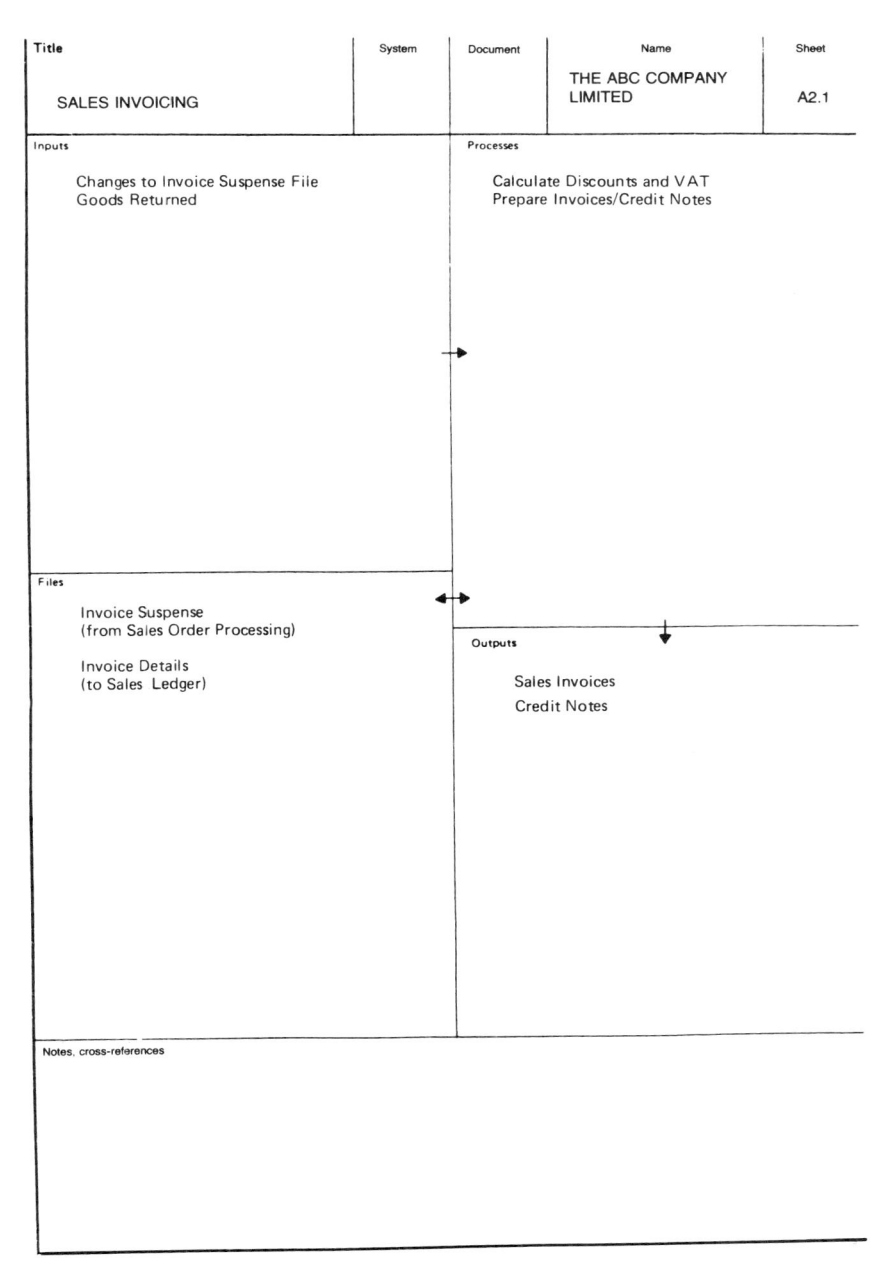

Title	System	Document	Name	Sheet
SALES INVOICING			THE ABC COMPANY LIMITED	A2.1

Inputs

　　Changes to Invoice Suspense File
　　Goods Returned

Processes

　　Calculate Discounts and VAT
　　Prepare Invoices/Credit Notes

Files

　　Invoice Suspense
　　(from Sales Order Processing)

　　Invoice Details
　　(to Sales Ledger)

Outputs

　　Sales Invoices
　　Credit Notes

Notes, cross-references

SALES INVOICING   **THE ABC COMPANY LTD**   A2.2

VOLUMES

Number of Sales Invoices per month:	5,000 ave	10,000 max
Number of lines per invoice	3 ave	30 max
Number of returns from customers per month:	100 ave	250 max

FORMS

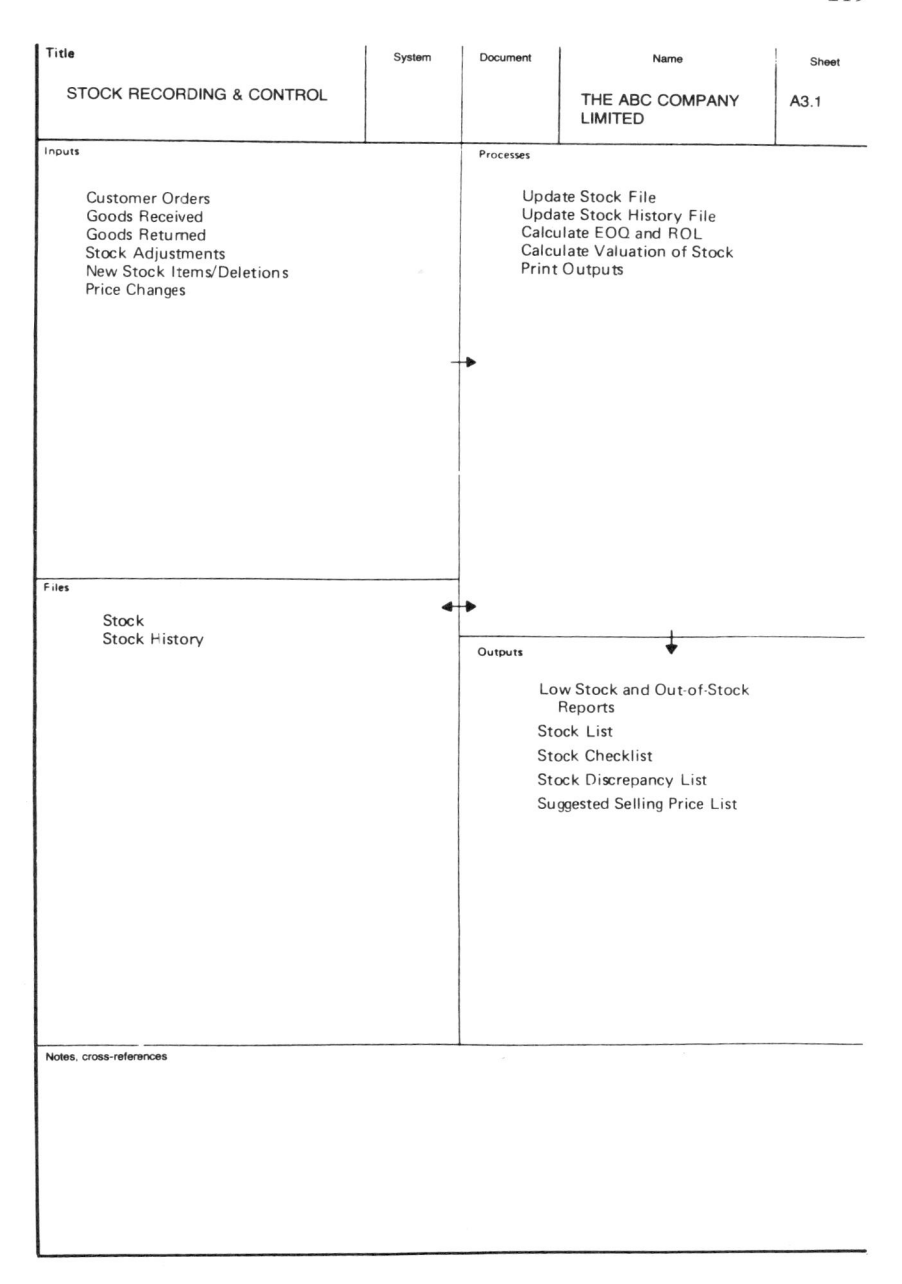

Title	System	Document	Name	Sheet
STOCK RECORDING & CONTROL			THE ABC COMPANY LIMITED	A3.1

Inputs

- Customer Orders
- Goods Received
- Goods Returned
- Stock Adjustments
- New Stock Items/Deletions
- Price Changes

Processes

- Update Stock File
- Update Stock History File
- Calculate EOQ and ROL
- Calculate Valuation of Stock
- Print Outputs

Files

- Stock
- Stock History

Outputs

- Low Stock and Out-of-Stock Reports
- Stock List
- Stock Checklist
- Stock Discrepancy List
- Suggested Selling Price List

Notes, cross-references

STOCK RECORDING AND CONTROL **THE ABC COMPANY LTD** A3.2

VOLUMES

Number of Stock Items:	2,000	
Number of transactions (issues and receipts) per month:		30,000 ave
Number of price changes per month:	10 min	1,000 max

FORMS

| **STOCK RECORDING AND CONTROL** | **THE ABC COMPANY LTD** | **A3.3** |

STOCK RECORD

	Product code	9(8)	
	Description	X(30)	
	Classification code	A	
	Unit of measure	A(4)	
	Storage location	9(2)	
	Physical stock quantity	9(5)	
	Quantity on order	9(5)	
	Quantity allocated	9(5)	
	Free stock	9(5)	
	Re-order level	9(5)	
	Lead time	9(5)	
	Economic order quantity	9(5)	
	Supplier's min order quantity	9(5)	
Occurs for each	Date	9(6)	DDMMYY
receipt into stock.	Unit cost price	9(5)	
Max 4 per record.	Quantity received	9(5)	
Quantity debited on	Unit selling price	9(5)	
FIFO basis	VAT rate	9(3)	
	Supplier's code	X(8)	
	Date of last stock check	9(6)	DDMMYY
	Cumulative demand (4 months-Home)	9(6)	
	Cumulative demand (4 months-Export)	9(6)	
	Cumulative demand (annual value)	9(9)	

RECORD SIZE: Approx.   150 characters

FORMS

Title	System	Document	Name	Sheet
SALES LEDGER AND SALES ANALYSIS			THE ABC COMPANY LIMITED	A4.1

Inputs

Credit Notes
Remittance Details
Adjustments

Processes

Maintain Files
Print Outputs

Files

Invoice Details
(from Sales Invoicing)
Sales Ledger
Representative Details

Outputs

(All produced monthly)

Statements
Overdue Accounts
Aged Debt
Representatives
Commission Report

Notes, cross-references

SALES LEDGER AND   **THE ABC COMPANY LTD**   A4.2
SALES ANALYSIS

VOLUMES

Number of customers	2,500
Number of statements per month	1,800
Number of representatives	25

SALES LEDGER AND SALES ANALYSIS	THE ABC COMPANY LTD		A4.3

SALES LEDGER RECORD

Customer account number	9(8)	
Name and address	4 x X (25)	
Telephone number	9(15)	
Telex number	9(10)	
Credit limit	9(5)	
Current month's invoices	9(7)	
1 month	9(7)	
2 months	9(7)	
3 months	9(7)	
Over 3 months	9(8)	
Total outstanding balance	9(8)	
Sales value year to date	9(8)	

occurs for each invoice until cleared:

Invoice number	9(6)	
Invoice date	9(6)	DDMMYY
Invoice amount	9(5)	
VAT amount	9(4)	

RECORD SIZE: Approx.   250 characters

SALES LEDGER THE ABC COMPANY LTD A4.4

REPRESENTATIVE RECORD

	Rep code	9(3)
	Commission Rate	9
occurs for	Invoice number	9(6)
this month's	Item amount (occurs for each item on	9(5)
invoices	the invoice	

RECORD SIZE: Approx.   800 characters

FORMS

Title	System	Document	Name	Sheet
PURCHASE ORDER MONITORING			THE ABC COMPANY LIMITED	A5.1

Inputs

Purchase Orders
Purchase Invoices

Processes

Update Outstanding Purchase Order File
Update Purchase Invoice Pending File

Files

Outstanding Purchase Order
Purchase Invoice Pending
(to Purchase Ledger)

Outputs

Value of Outstanding Orders Report
(on request)

Notes, cross-references

PURCHASE ORDER MONITORING   **THE ABC COMPANY LTD**   A5.2

VOLUMES

Number of suppliers	510	
Number of purchase orders per month	600 ave	1,000 max
Number of purchase invoices per month	1,000 ave	1,500 max

FORMS

Title	System	Document	Name	Sheet
PURCHASE LEDGER AND PURCHASE ANALYSIS			THE ABC COMPANY LIMITED	A6.1

Inputs

Credit Notes
Supplier Details/Amendments

Processes

Maintain File
Print Outputs

Files

Purchase Invoice Pending
(from Purchase Order Monitoring)
Purchase Ledger

Outputs

(All produced monthly)

Payments List
Remittance Advices
Purchase Analyses

Notes, cross-references

PURCHASE LEDGER AND   **THE ABC COMPANY LTD**   **A6.2**
PURCHASE ANALYSIS

VOLUMES

Number of Suppliers	510	
Number of purchase invoices per month	1,000 ave	1,500 max
Number of payments per month	100 ave	

FORMS

PURCHASE LEDGER AND PURCHASE ANALYSIS   **THE ABC COMPANY LTD**   A6.3

PURCHASE LEDGER RECORD

	Suppliers account code	9(6)	
	Name and address	4 × X(25)	
	Account balance	9(7)	
	Turnover for current month	9(7)	
	Turnover year-to-date	9(8)	
	Turnover for previous year	9(8)	
	Number of orders placed	9(4)	
occurs for each	Purchase invoice number	9(6)	
invoice	Invoice date	9(6)	DDMMYY
until cleared	Invoice amount	9(6)	

RECORD SIZE: Approx.   200 characters

FORMS

Title	System	Document	Name	Sheet
NOMINAL LEDGER			THE ABC COMPANY LIMITED	A7.1

Inputs

Budget for each
Account Code
Monthly Postings

Processes

Maintain File
Print Outputs

Files

Nominal Ledger

Outputs

Trial Balance per month
Budget Comparisons

Notes, cross-references

NOMINAL LEDGER   **THE ABC COMPANY LTD**   A7.2

VOLUMES

Number of accounts   270

Number of postings per month   580 ave

NOMINAL LEDGER   **THE ABC COMPANY LTD**   A7.3

NOMINAL LEDGER RECORD

Account Code	9(3)
Description	X(25)
Current account balance	9(9)
Cumulative to date	9(9)
Budget	9(9)
Build up of total by month	12 x 9(7)

RECORD SIZE: Approx.   120 characters

FORMS

Title	System	Document	Name	Sheet
PAYROLL			THE ABC COMPANY LIMITED	A8.1

Inputs

    Clock Cards
    New Starters
    Leavers
    Amendments

Processes

    Maintain File
    Calculate Gross Pay,
    Tax and Deductions
    Preparation of Payslip

Files

    Payroll

Outputs

    Payslips
    Cash Analysis
    NHI and Tax Returns
    Year End Analysis

Notes, cross-references

PAYROLL   **THE ABC COMPANY LTD**   **A8.2**

VOLUMES

Number of hourly paid employees	120
Number of weekly paid employees	30
Number of monthly paid employees	30

FORMS

PAYROLL
PAYROLL RECORD
THE ABC COMPANY LTD
A8.3

Employee number	X(4)
Employee name	X(25)
Hourly rate	9(4)
Overtime rate	9(4)
Superannuation	9(6)
Tax Code	9(4)
NHI number	9(9)
Standard Deductions	
— NHI	
— Pension	
— Saving Scheme	
— etc.	6 x 9(4)
Gross pay to date	9(6)
Tax to date	9(5)

RECORD SIZE: Approx. 100 characters

APPENDIX 6

Glossary of Terms

GLOSSARY

Access time	– The time that elapses between the moment the command to access a location or area is given, and the moment when the transfer of data to or from that area can commence.
Acoustic coupler	– A data communications device which enables a digital signal to be transmitted over the telephone network using an ordinary telephone handset.
Applications software	– A set of specialised programs and associated documentation to carry out a task (such as Stock Control).
Assembler	– A program which translates a program written in symbolic language into machine or object language.
Backing store	– A large capacity data store supplementing the central store and accessible by CPU command.
Batch processing	– An approach to processing where similar input items are grouped for processing during the same machine run.
Binary	– The number representation system with a base of two, ie using only digits 0 and 1.
Bit	– A binary digit.
Block	– A set of data which is of a convenient size to handle as a single unit of transfer between CPU and peripheral device.
Bureau	– A company which sells processing time on its computer system.
CPU	– Central Processing Unit. The main part of the computer consisting of the central store, arithmetic unit and control unit.
Chip	– A very small piece of silicon in which one or more electronic components have been formed.

Compiler — A program which translates a source program written in a high-level language into a computer's machine code. Each high-level language instruction is changed into several machine-code instructions.

Computer — A machine which, under the control of a stored program, automatically accepts and processes data and supplies the results of that processing.

Cycle time — The time interval between the start and restart of a particular hardware operation.

Data — Information coded in a form acceptable for input to and processing by a computer system.

Data communications — The transmission of data between the user and the computer.

Digital computer — A computer where data is represented by combinations of discrete pulses denoted by 0s and 1s.

Disk — A storage device consisting of a flat rotatable circular plate coated on both surfaces with a magnetic material. Data is written to and read from a set of concentric circular tracks.

Disk drive — The mechanism which causes the movement of the disks between the sensing or writing mechanisms.

Disk pack — A set of disks arranged a fixed distance apart on a common central spindle.

Disk unit — A peripheral device consisting of a magnetic disk or disks and the associated read/write and drive mechanisms.

GLOSSARY

File	– An organised collection of related records.
Hardware	– The physical units from which a computer is built; the mechanical, magnetic, electrical and electronic devices of a computer.
Implementation	– The series of operations putting the system into effect, terminating in its live running on a computer. Includes detailed system design, programming, file creation, testing and changeover.
Key-to-disk	– A data collection system where information is input via terminals and stored on disk suitably batched for later input to a computer system.
Line driver	– An amplifier used to transmit analogue or digital signals over a transmission line or circuit.
Memory	– Part of a computer where data and instructions are held.
Modem	– MOdulator/DEModulator. A device to allow the conversion of bits into analogue electrical impulses for transmission over telephone type circuits, and vice versa.
Object code	– The translated version of a program which has been processed by the assembler or compiler.
On-line	– Equipment, devices and systems in direct interactive communication with the CPU.
On-line processing	– Processing performed on equipment directly under the control of the central processor whilst the user remains in communication with the computer.

Operating console — An input/output device which consists of a keyboard with a printer or a VDU. It is used by the computer operator to control the computer.

Operating system — A complex software system which controls the operation of the computer system and relieves the human operator of much of the detailed work. Normally it will include a complicated scheduling and loading program to ensure optimum utilisation of the available equipment.

Peripheral — Term used to describe any input, output or backup storage device which can be connected to the central processing unit.

Program — The complete sequence of instructions for a job to be performed on a computer.

Programming language — An artificial language established as a set of key words and the syntax rules for combining these words, with which a programmer may instruct the computer to perform tasks.

Punched card — A rectangular card in which data is recorded by punching patterns of holes in a recognised code.

Record — A collection of associated items of data which together form an element of a file, eg a stock record, a customer record.

Register — A high-speed device used in a central processing unit for temporary storage of small amounts of data or intermittent results during processing.

Software — Refers to all programs which a user has available for use on his machine whether written by his own programmers or by outside organisations.

GLOSSARY

Software house — A commercial organisation which specialises in the preparation of application packages and tailor-made programs for other organisations.

Source code — A program as written by the programmer in a programming language. It must be assembled or compiled before it can be run.

Storage — A general term covering all units of computer equipment used to store data including programs and instructions.

Systems software — The collection of programs available for the total control of the performance of a computer system.

Terminal — A device such as a key-driven or visual display terminal which can be connected to a computer over a communications circuit and which may be used for either input or output from a location either near or far removed the computer.

Turnkey system — A computer system supplied as a complete package of hardware and software to support the required applications.

VDU — Visual Display Unit. A terminal device equipped with a television-type screen, eg a cathode ray tube, and a keyboard, thus permitting data to be displayed on a screen and providing facilities for the operator to input data to the system via the keyboard.

Verification — The process of checking the accuracy of data.